GW00459105

EYES FOR THE INVISIBLE

Dedicated to the Reverend Ciarán Woods,
Diocese of Clogher
Died April 6th 1993, Holy Week

Patrick McCafferty

Eyes for the Invisible
THE GIFT OF FAITH IN OUR TIME

the columba press

First edition 1994 published by
Τhe columba press
93 The Rise, Mount Merrion, Blackrock, Co Dublin

Cover by Bill Bolger
Origination by The Columba Press
Printed in Ireland by
Genprint Ltd, Dublin

ISBN 1 85607 094 8

Copyright © 1994, Patrick McCafferty

Contents

PRELUDE: 'Even the angels long to have a glimpse of these things'
(1 Pet 1:12).   8

1. A crisis of faith: A question of identity   13

2. The living and true God: Goal of the human journey   23

3. Discipleship: Life from a cross and resurrection perspective 37

4. The mystery of faith: Ultimate presence   53

5. God among us: A real and abiding presence   62

6. Communion and action: Becoming what we receive   71

7. Prayer: Loving a passionate God   82

8. Mary: Transfigured humanity personified   91

POSTLUDE: 'For our God is a consuming fire' (Heb 12:29).   103

And so we have no eyes for things that are visible
but only for the invisible,
for the visible things last only for a while
and the invisible things are eternal
2 Cor 4:18

'Even the angels long to catch a glimpse of these things'
Peter 1:12

Faith is the path along which we approach our God whom we cannot see. On this way therefore, there is nothing known to the senses: we are in the domain of what 'no eye has seen and no ear has heard, things beyond the mind of any person, all that God has prepared for those who love him' (1 Cor 2:9). It is in this atmosphere of faith that the earthly Church acts, lives and breathes. The gift of faith is of the very essence of the disciples relating to an invisible, yet really present God. To believe is the fundamental vocation of a Christian. With this brand of belief, however, there must be nothing of a passive or vegetative state; for this way of faith is a whole manner of living which engages our entire person in a relationship that is active, dynamic and passionate.

Faith, therefore, is a friendship; it is keeping the Lord ever in our sight (Ps 16:2). But because faith is a radically new way of looking and seeing, it will be necessary to search for God in the not so obvious places, in regions unexplored. To find God, one must look into the depths of life and living; for it is there, beneath the surface of reality, that we will meet God who loves us with a passion. If he hides his glory from us now, it is purely out of tender regard and thoughtful consideration for the present delicate state of our humanity.

The Word which awakens faith coaxes gently and falls upon our human nature like a soft, yet persistent, rain. God warms the seed of endless life sown within us, with the breath of his presence, until the colours of transfigured glory are ripe to unfurl; when eventually, our present perishable nature will put on imperishability and our mortal nature, immortality (1 Cor 15:53).

Faith is a voyage of discovery, an adventure on which we set out to explore hidden realities. The navigator on our quest is the Spirit we have received from the risen Christ. This is the Spirit who explores the depths of everything, even the depths of God (1 Cor 2:11). The Spirit, who has made a home in us, unwraps for us the gift of all gifts, for he unveils the presence of God among us. We can only but be filled with a sense of wonder and awe as the eternal draws near to us and begins to express himself in palpable form, unveiling his name and nature at the appropriate time as Emmanuel – I am with you always!

There unfolds before the eyes of faith, the realisation that at every instant of our existing he is present to us and we to him. The Psalmist expresses it thus: 'Close behind and close in front you fence me round, shielding me with your hand' (Ps 139:5). Indeed, well and truly might we not say, along with the thunderstruck author of Psalm 8:

> I look up at your heavens, made by your fingers, at the moon and stars you set in place – ah! what are human beings that you should spare thought for them, mere mortals that you should care for them? (Ps 8:3-4).

Yes, the human person, man and woman, is his work of art (Eph 2:10): the ultimate manifestation of God's creative genius as love. As does the artist on canvas and the composer on manuscript, so too does God express who he is, in creating us. We were conceived in his heart as a most loving thought. He fashioned and formed us as the *pièce de resistance* of that overflowing generosity and goodness, which is concretised in his giving us life. In such love do we have our origins – the roots of our existence. We are given life because we are loved by God and called to be people who love. It is in loving relationship with our creator Father and with one another, that we discover the fullness of life.

To have eyes for the invisible is to learn to see with faith and so be confronted by the passionate God who is true to his name – Emmanuel, God in our midst. To see the invisible is to contemplate God who lies hidden from our senses and to adore him present at the heart of our living. It is by faith that he desires to encounter us, heart to heart, face to face. This feat of love is achieved by the sending among us of he who is the Father's intimate and nearest his heart (Jn 1:18). The beloved Son is infinitely qualified to tell us all about the Father and to be the bearer of his overtures of love and reconciliation for humanity: 'for on him, the Father, God himself, has set his seal' (Jn 6:27).

Christ is the priest who admits us to that holy and secret place, where God waits to keep tryst with us. Christ is the prophet of the invisible who calls the Church into being and walks with us towards the hidden reality of the kingdom. Christ is the king and head of the Church which is his body (Col 1:18). Therefore, in him, we are able to reach up and touch the mystery of Love that is God. In Christ, we are caught up in his fiery embrace.

Much of our modern age is deprived of beauty and starved of mystery. It is, therefore , an ever more vital aspect of our Christian vocation to have a vision of reality that transcends the horizon of the merely material and purely perceptible. For there remains always a burning thirst at the core of every human life:

> As a deer longs for running streams, so longs my soul for you, my God. My soul thirsts for God, the God of life; When shall I go to see the face of God? (Ps 42:1-2).

Nothing less than the real God, the living God, can quench such a desire. 'When shall I go to see the face of God?' Psalm 42 is the song of a pilgrim who is homesick with longing for the temple in Jerusalem, the place where, it was believed, God dwelt. In our own day, however, the apostle Paul asks us this question: 'Didn't you realise that you were God's temple and that the Spirit of God was living among you?' (1 Cor 3:16-17). Christ, in opening our eyes to God's presence among us, to the fact that *we* are that temple, makes us aware that we are daughters and sons of the Father and therefore, sisters and brothers of one another.

His mission is to tell us who we are. His gospel is the good news of the truth about you and me – we are loved by God. Our dignity and worth is the direct result of his loving us passionately. In the difficult surroundings of today's increasingly anti-human and soulless environments, the Church enshrines and proclaims that truth. The Church, after all, is people. It is in our flesh, bones and blood that God is enshrined, in our hearts has he made his home; and with the raw materials of our lives, he can, in fact, construct 'a kingdom of holiness and grace, a kingdom of truth and life, a kingdom of justice, love and peace' (*Preface of Christ the King*).

In company with Christ, in whom we see our God made visible, we approach the threshold of the kingdom and stand on the doorstep of mystery. And so already, by faith, we catch a glimpse of what no eye has seen; we can sense an echo of what no ear has heard; we are given an inkling, albeit vague and faint, of the welcome God has made ready for those who love him.

This can happen because, in Christ, God has come centre stage in the human drama. Through Christ, with him and in him, God has access to all areas of life and living. He comes to dwell in the hearts of all who believe, who hope and who love; he has put down roots in our human flesh and blood and flooded all created reality with his loving presence.

CHAPTER ONE

A crisis of faith: A question of identity

The gift of Faith in our time

We are approaching the threshold of the twenty-first century AD and, in a sense, Christianity is about to come to age. Yet it is plainly obvious that humanity, certainly in the western hemisphere, is in the throes of a crisis of faith: a crisis that is manifest not merely in dwindling congregations, for emptying churches are but a symptom of a far more extensive ailment.

Some indeed may very well be voting with their feet and abandoning religious practice as an expression of disappointment and disillusionment with the institutional Church. What is certain, however, is that human beings are still hungry for substantial spiritual food and thirsty for encounter with the eternal. For example, there abounds and multiplies today, an assortment of religious sects and cults which are becoming increasingly bizarre in their claims and counter claims. The real danger exists whereby the human person's inate religious sense could become distorted in a haze of emotional excitement and fleeting fervour. From a Christian perspective in particular, genuine religious belief, along with its communal implications, becomes diverted into a maze of fruitless individualism and esoteric elitism. Our problem therefore, would seem to be, not only a crisis of faith but, in reality, a dilemma of identity, an amnesia of the human spirit.

The present day difficulties being encountered by Churches, in making the gospel challenge and the call to Christian discipleship comprehensible to contemporary men and women, is experienced, more often than not, in a growing indifference and an apathetic shrug of the shoulders, rather than outright hostility or rejection. Perhaps the modern 'so what' as opposed to 'Amen', stems to some degree from the situation where, for well over a century of the modern era, human beings have been raised on a staple diet of the purely perceptible and merely material. Reality has been defined solely in empirical terms; as only that which is experiential and knowable, in so far as the senses are concerned. Therefore, because faith treats of realities hidden and sights unseen, more and more people are scratching their heads in bewilderment, when faced with the language and symbols of belief.

From a pastoral point of view, what we must contend with is the scenario of men and women reeling in a daze from the constant bombardment, assault and battery of their sense nature. Our present difficulties in the area of faith arise out of an incomplete and indeed falsified picture of the human person. People, for example, are termed 'punters' and viewed as valuable only in so far as they contribute or consume, in the overall scheme of buying and producing. Such a philosophy and understanding of the human person, divorces men and women from any significant spiritual context. Thus human beings are plundered of their true dignity, status and significance.

This situation arises out of ever-expanding empires, founded upon principles of expediency and materialism, promiscuity and hedonism. A climate of deprivation begins to prevail and an environment created in which people lose the sense of who they really are. We can almost begin to define ourselves solely in physical and material terms and forget that God has created us with the potential to reach into eternity. And so, it becomes harder to have eyes for the invisible and to see the hidden realities of faith. Much of the various media now at the disposal of society, constantly assail the senses and seduce the spirit with the alluring rationale of self-indulgence. The community of faith, on the verge of the third millennium, is certainly faced with a daunting challenge. So how are we to react and what do we do?

When it comes to the business of engaging and confounding these forces that militate against humanity, we are far from ill-equipped. The apostle Paul's advice is, in this context, as timely and relevant as ever:

> Put God's armour on ... For it is not against human enemies that we have to struggle, but against the sovereignties and the powers who originate the darkness in this world, the spiritual

army of evil in the heavens. That is why you must rely on God's armour, or you will not be able to put up any resistance when the worst happens, or have enough resources to hold your ground (Eph 6:10-13).

As always, it is the spirit who is at work in the rebellious, (Eph 1:1), who pervades any scheme, the purpose of which is, the ultimate undermining of God's purpose and his desire for humanity.

And so, Paul goes on to counsel the family of faith in every age:

So stand your ground with truth buckled round your waist, and integrity for a breastplate, wearing for shoes on your feet the eagerness to spread the gospel of peace. And always carrying the shield of faith so that you can use it to put out the burning arrows of the evil one (Eph 6:1-17).

In every era and epoch of human history and experience, when faced by problems from within and without, the Church is always, in a spiritual sense, armed to the teeth with the gospel of peace. For this gospel is the good news of the truth, in regard to who God is and who we are, in relation to him; as created, loved and valued by him. The Church's brief from the risen Lord and the mission of the individual disciple, is to uphold that truth and live by it. For it is the good news of our intrinsic worth as human beings: a proclamation of the unalterable fact that every man, woman and child is eternally relevant to God and precious in his eyes.

The Church, at its beginning, was entrusted with this news of immense joy. It was empowered and authorised by the risen Christ, to go to the afflicted. There is a real sense in which we need to speak once more with the vibrancy of our youthful faith; for the gospel of Christ is vehemently and dogmatically affirmative of our humanity. Beautiful once more must be the very sound of the steps of those who bear within them, like a burning fire, the message of God drawing near to and consoling his people. The gospel's joyous strains must, once more, become music to the ears of those who are aimless and wandering, those alienated, those crushed and broken by their experiences of living. The message of Christ can be light to the eyes of those blinded to their true worth and dignity; for it is the favourable verdict from the very heart of God, which brings to an end the sentence of the despairing. The community of faith is enlivened and 'en-Spirited' by Christ, to proclaim God's favour; the unending amnesty of his love to all who will welcome the Word with joyful generosity.

Christ himself, of course, is that Word addressed to us by the Father, in which he says: 'I am with you'. Christ's presence among us is the ultimate gesture of affirmation, by God, of our humanity. Through Christ, with him and in him, we are given the right to reclaim our lost place in the midst of creation, even though this place of honour was foolishly, yet freely, abandoned by humanity in the first place. However, such undeserved affirmation and unmerited solidarity on God's behalf, is the whole wonder of love expressed in the Lord's cross and resurrection. For it is there that we meet God standing beside us in the darkness of our pain, in our sensation of being lost and abandoned, in our loneliness in the face of death. What is referred to as the paschal mystery is nothing less that the full reality of Christ, who says to us: 'Fear not, I am here. Yes it is I. Do not be afraid.' It is he who catches hold of us with his almighty arm and walks us through our experience of defeat and dying, into the super abundant, endless life of the resurrected.

The gospel challenge invites us always to a more radical commitment and a deeper fidelity, to the truth of who we are and why we are. That truth we see revealed in the life of Christ; he bears witness to it in his passion and death and vindicates it forever in his resurrection and ascension. In stating that truth, Christ directs our gaze beyond the surface of life and living, towards a reality that is not in any way perceptible or obvious to the senses. For God wills to meet us and for us to come to know him, not in the shallow waters of the merely material, but at the very heart of reality and in the depths of our beings. He desires to speak with us heart to heart and for us to commune with him as the profound and utter reality: as the one in whom we live and move and have our being (Acts 17:28).

The mystery of faith, proclaimed in Christian living and praying, is the fact of God's being with us in solidarity and communion. His Spirit, which fills the universe with the breath of life, is the flame that burns at the centre of our human existence. This truth is well expressed by the Psalmist:

> ... you stop their breath, they die and revert to dust. You give breath, fresh life begins, you keep renewing the world (Ps 104:29-30).

The mission God has given to the Church – the family of all who believe – is to follow the Spirit's joyful dance across time and throughout the ages, into the new heavens and the new earth. The life lived by faith, is a setting out upon an adventure of love, illumined by that dancing fire whose name is the joyful Spirit – the Lord the giver of life! The life of faith is a digging deep towards the centre of our being and thus a discovery of real and enduring riches. To put it simply, believing is being in love with God.

To believe is to have a trained eye for the invisible fact of his being with us; it is to have an ear finely tuned to the silent sound of his step and the secret ways of his approaches to us. Prayer is loving and being loved by God: the believer must be a student of that wordless language of the heart and therefore a connoisseur of the hidden things of God. The disciple strives to live in the knowledge that '... now the life you have is hidden with Christ in God (Col 3:3).

The Christian life, in its totality, is a continuous proclaiming of the mystery of faith – the paschal mystery of our Lord's life, death and glorification – which is the means of our sharing in the fullness of God's life. Our life now, therefore, is 'a life lived in Christ, rooted in him and built upon him, held firm by the faith we have been taught, and over flowing with thanksgiving' (Col 2:7). It is therefore, a eucharistic life. Our faith-life must, by its very nature, be an ongoing making present of the God who is with us and always for us. A God whose loving invitation is ever in the present tense; who makes possible for all who will respond in faith, the perennial opportunity of a life enriched by graced potential. A God whose answer to men and women is eternally 'Yes!' and always, 'Now!'

Rediscovering our origins

Much of our present difficulty in relation to faith stems largely from the exaltation of the sensual and material as the alpha and omega of reality. It is therefore necessary to keep in mind, the divine meaning of our humanity. We are much more than mere flesh and blood. Our physical being is like the husk of a seed that will germinate into eternal growth and fecundity. Christ opens our eyes to this wonder, this marvel that the Lord, who invests our being with the Spirit of life, works for us.

Who am I? Why am I? It is as important today as ever, to ask ourselves these fundamental questions. We need to go back to our roots to, rediscover the answer. Perhaps a little research at the Public Records Office will help.

As far as our faith story goes, the record of our human origins and beginnings, is contained in the book of Genesis. The opening chapter of Genesis relates, in intelligible story form, how when God created the heavens and the earth, the earth was a formless void and that there was darkness over the waters. So what we have to begin with is a scene of chaos, absurdity and confusion. Already, however, a breath of life was stirring and making ripples over the dark waters. Such is our introduction to that Spirit often referred to in scripture as the breath of God.

The sacred authors of Genesis, under the guidance of that same creator Spirit, have constructed out of borrowed creation myths and legends of the ancient world, a shrine for truth. The truth that, in the beginning, at the dawn of the created order, when reality was in the throes of birth, God is present nursing all things into being. He brings forth harmony out of chaos and disarray; where there is only a vacuum of non-entity, he creates life and existence. Then, at the crescendo of God's spectacular improvisation on a theme of dust and nothingness, there comes the master stroke:

> God created the human person in the image of himself, in the image of God he created them, male and female he created them (Gen 1:27).

God shaped the first human being from the soil of the ground and blew the breath of life into his nostrils, and the human person thus became a living being (Gen 2:7). The kiss of the creator Spirit awakens humanity to existence.

When preparing to execute this master-work of creating man and woman, God said: 'Let us make the human person in our own image, in the likeness of ourselves ... (Gen 1:26). And so, we can discover the basic truth about man and woman: we exist for the purpose of relationship and communion, with the one who created us and with one another. This reality is reflected and expressed in our nature as familial, societal, relationship-forming beings.

When we go back to our roots, we discover that throughout all the millions of years that the universe has been in existence, the Spirit of God has been active in a painstaking labour of love: the craft of gradually forming and constructing the cosmos; likewise, throughout all the long millenia of human generations and amidst all the twists and turns of our history, that same Spirit has been at work in calling human beings to realise the true purpose of their existence; to share, ever more deeply and intimately, in God's friendship. Our God has told us that his name is Love (1Jn 4:7-8). He loves us into life, that he might share his glory and happiness with us, in eternal companionship. He invites us to respond to him in love. We accept his gift of life and so realise the full potential of our existence, by becoming and being, people who love.

God: Trinity, relationship and community
We exist in the image and likeness of God: a God who has revealed the divine nature as an interacting communion of love; as creative and dynamic; as infinite goodness and generosity who loves to give joyful expression to that nature. The doctrine of the Holy Trinity unfolded very early in the Church's contemplation of the mystery of God. It is an attempt to express what is essentially inexpressible. Yet the truth of this teaching gives us a glimpse of the inner life of the God who creates us and who cradles us in the arms of his living love. This God of ours is, of his very essence, an active and loving relationship – a communion of Father, Son and Holy Spirit. God is a companionship that is dynamic, creative and life-giving.

Let us attempt for a moment to exercise what are, for this particular task, rather inadequate imaginations; for we are daring to visualise what no eye has seen and no mind can begin to grasp.

God is love. Love is something that cannot possibly ever be merely an idea or a concept. It demands expression and indeed, craves tangible manifestation, by its very nature. From all eternity, therefore, before ever the world was or the ages began, the Father is present. He is Life and Love. In order to express that Love, he speaks a Word – Son. The Son is the fruit of the Father's loving from all eternity. The Son is not created by the Father anymore than an apple is created by the tree: trees do not make fruit, they simply fulfil their potential by bearing it. And so the Son comes from the Father's heart. He is therefore, begotten not made, of one being with the Father. He is God from God, Light from Light, Fire from Fire, true God from true God.

The Father and the Son are one. The Father loves the Son and the Son loves the Father. And the power and intensity of that unfathomable love is made present in the Holy Spirit. The Holy Spirit breathes the divine life into creation; the Spirit animates and motivates; it is the Spirit who moulds and shapes reality according to God's purpose. The Holy Spirit is the eternal wisdom who conceives God's loving plans and brings them to fruition.

The Holy Spirit is mysterious but she is not some form of vague willowy presence. She is quite tangible. To what can she be compared? She is like the warmth of love that exists among friends and families. She is like a cool breeze on a hot and sultry day; like the quiet breath of an infant asleep; like the full vent of a furious wind. She can be likened to a sparkling and bubbling brook of crystal-clear water. She is colour and light. She leaps and dances in youthful limbs.

She consoles like the tender caresses of a mother and father. Her voice is like the sage advice expressed by those who have lived long and learnt much. Yet the Spirit of the Lord can be daring and bold as any hot-blooded teenager, full of enthusiasm and zeal for life.

The Holy Spirit, the Lord, the Giver of Life moves our hearts to respond thus to our passionate and loving God:

> Come in, let us bow, prostrate ourselves, and kneel in front of the Lord our maker, for this is our God, and we are the people he pastures, the flock he guides (Ps 95:6-7).

From all eternity therefore, God is three persons united in one communion of love. From all time, God's heart desires that the human person he created, take up the place he has prepared for us, in the family circle of the Trinity. The Holy Trinity, in creating us, made room for us at their table of hospitality. God has made ready a feast of eternal delight which will fill us with endless life and happiness.

Such is the God who created us and who loves us. We know too, however, from the record of our beginnings in Genesis, how man and woman freely co-operated with a scheme which resulted in their being swindled and stripped, of all the rich gifts God had originally presented them with. By their own choice they had thrown it all away. They had gambled and lost. Having believed a liar, they had exchanged their pass to endless companionship with the God who had given them life, for a counterfeit certificate that promised all happiness. Had God's name been anything other than Love, then he could have, justifiably, turned his back on us. He could have rightly cast us away from his presence and deprived us forever of his Spirit of Life (cf Ps 51:11).

How, however, could the heart of God fail to be moved, at the sorry plight of men and women whom he created for no other reason than that he loved them with a passion? Love would find a way to give back what he had been thrown away. The ingenuity of eternal love would not fail to mastermind a way by which to bring us back. And what a way indeed!

It is to realise God's desire that we find him again, that Christ comes into the world at the appointed time. Christ arrives, filled with the Holy Spirit, to set in motion and bring to completion the task of renovating and restoring our humanity. He is come to bring us back to the friendship and love of the Father, revesting us with the original dignity thrown off by the human race, at the time of the first sin.

Christ, because he is the only Son who is nearest the Father's heart (Jn 1:18), is well qualified to describe the real and living God, to actually enflesh his presence among us and make him known. He is the Word and, therefore, the visible and tangible expression of the Father's life and love, living among us in flesh and blood. This truth is well expressed, in strikingly beautiful language, by the apostle John at the beginning of his first epistle:

> Something which has existed since the beginning, which we have heard, which we have seen with our own eyes, which we have watched and touched with our hands, the word of life – this is our theme. That life was made visible; we saw it and are giving our testimony, declaring to you the eternal life which was present to the Father and has been revealed to us (Jn 1:1-2).

Yes, it is life that has been revealed to us. God can never again be relegated to the outer heavens or exiled to the sphere of ideas and vague probabilities. In Christ, the glory has dawned upon us and for ever, of that true light which enlightens all men and women (Jn 1:9).

God is real and his life has, in Christ, been made visible. We can touch it and experience its fullness. Through Jesus Christ, who becomes a human being, God embraces humanity and welcomes men and women into his inner life – into the family circle of the Trinity.

The contemporary crisis of belief is an opportunity to be seized by people of faith. A chance to restate the great truths of the Christian faith with all the clarity and conviction that their beauty, ever ancient and ever new, demands. For their source is the real and living God who has, in Christ the Word made flesh, firmly planted himself in the midst of our human living and experience.

The heralding of the truth, however, must never be the flag-waving exercise of an exclusive and triumphalistic Church. The source of revealed truth cannot be fathomed or contained in anyone's equation nor even in a million books. His embrace is wide enough for the entire human race, in all its diversity of opinion and practice. He is able to accompany all who search along the many avenues of their journeys. The community of faith must approach the men and women of today with a genuinely compassionate desire to be of service; with a passion for dialogue and debate, tempered with respectful regard for the integrity of the beliefs of others; and with a concern to provide an effective and contemporary lexicon of faith, which will provide for this day and age, a worthy vehicle for the truth revealed in Jesus Christ.

CHAPTER TWO

The living and true God: Goal of the human journey

The first sin and its consequences
A by-product of the first sin, or fall, has been a certain shame-faced shyness on the part of humanity when it comes to approaching the Divine. The first man and woman hid from God, conscious for the first time of their nakedness after they had betrayed him, and allowed themselves to be betrayed by the serpent's craft. Thus it was that the human race took cover from the reality of the Divine Presence; and in doing so, enmeshed itself in a net of self-justification, self-preservation and self-deception. Among the first casualties of the fall were compassion and communion. We witness a primeval pointing of the finger of blame: 'It was the woman's fault; she gave me the fruit and I ate it! The serpent tempted me and I ate.' God himself does not escape: 'It was the woman *you* put me with...' (cf. Gen 3: 8-13) The rounds of accusations have not ceased to make waves and ripples that wend their way throughout our history.

The doctrine of the original sin reflects upon and makes sense of, the mystery of unease and disorder that we discover in our own hearts and lives; that is virulent and active among communities and nations; and that seems to disturb and wound the very cosmos, as unpredictable and untameable forces of nature appear to mirror the distress of the human condition, and wreak havoc of inexplicable tragedy in the lives of human beings trying to work out their existence. It is a mystery of alienation that manifests itself in a malignant and fatal selfishness. The first or original sin could be likened to a gash inflicted in the early infancy of humanity. It was a blow invited by the courting of the strange serpent – the ancient foe and trickster – who harbours a profound and furious enmity for women and men, on account of the extent to which God loves them. The opening chapters of Genesis enshrine the truth of humanity's down-fallenness, in order to give an explanation for our sorry state and allow a prognosis to be formulated.

One could compare the plight of humanity to that of a shattered or wrenched limb: the man and his wife had believed the serpent-tempter and freely given their trust to him; the serpent, in gaining the ear of the human race, had used his wiles to catch hold of them, wrenching them suddenly away from God, shattering in the process, the original harmony, innocence and state of glory that they enjoyed with God in the beginning. St Paul expresses this mysterious fall from grace in the epistle to the Romans:

> Sin entered the world through one man, and through sin death, and thus death has spread through the whole human race because everyone has sinned. (Rom 5: 12)

The enemy of humanity, described by the Word of God as a murderer from the start and the father of lies (Jn 8: 33), invited the human race to fall; and in that falling from the heights of our intimacy with God, we were profoundly wounded in our nature. The repercussions of this fall have produced bitter fruit from generation to generation, causing the entire human family to be fractured, fragmented, and infected with death as a result of sin. Thus death has spread through the whole human race, shrouding everything, blighting our relationship with God and one another, and with the earth itself. The pain of the fall makes itself obvious in patterns of behaviour that are destructive of harmony and community and as modes of acting that are motivated by self-hatred. Sin that had now made its entrance into our world and experience, became the hereditary impediment to our rising again towards God, having been, communally and individually, knocked out of joint in our relationship to him.

So the man and woman went into exile. The human family wandered off to the four winds, away from the Garden of Life. At the end of the story of the fall in Genesis, however, there is mention of the posting of cherubs to guard the tree of life with flaming swords. (Gen 3: 24) This is a most thoughtful gesture on God's behalf, a Divine damage-limitation exercise. He also makes clothes for the man and woman to wear as a tender acknowledgement of their new-found limitations and frailty. The cherubs are sent to their posts to prevent further ravage being caused in an extremely delicate and vulnerable situation of raw pain. But already the way home is being mapped out in the Father's heart and God is preparing for his own pilgrimage in search of lost humanity. No sooner had the lethal wound been inflicted, no sooner had humanity stumbled off into the long night of alienation, than God began to make ready the great healing which would counteract the poison of death's sting.

He dreamt of it in his heart which was grieved at what had befallen his beloved daughters and sons; he set about preparing it with loving attention to the remotest detail, for it would be the means whereby he would bring us back from our exile in this dark vale of tears. The plan of salvation was conceived in the depths of God; the Father and the Son contemplated it together in the communion of the Spirit as they awaited the appointed time. The Spirit who is irrepressible Life and Love was animating the overtures of love from on high and guiding the intricate surgery of piecing together, once more, the fragmented masterpiece of God's hand. Diplomatic relations are not broken off and there begins a steady stream of ambassadors and emissaries, who lay the ground work of a reconciliation the like and extent of which no one, as yet, dared even to dream of; for its sure foundation will be a precious cornerstone of flesh and blood, one like ourselves though free from sin.

Human beings had been rendered incapable of enjoying the benefits of the tree of life through their rejection of the truth about themselves and the ready acceptance of a false analysis of their condition. For the serpent had said: *'No! You will not die! God knows in fact that on the day you eat it your eyes will be opened and you will be like gods, knowing good and evil.'* (Gen 3: 4-5) The original sin was a turning aside from the wisdom of God who had fashioned man and woman in his own likeness and according to his own design. This turning away from God that is sin, is similar to ignoring the instructions in a manufacturer's handbook when dealing with a complex mechanism; it is bound to result in harm being caused and damage having to be repaired. The only source of succour in such a situation would be the maker, as he will know his handiwork in all its intricacies and be able to restore and reconstruct what has been broken and misused.

This is the reason for the incarnation of the Word. He comes among us bearing the instructions from the Father's heart for our reconciliation with him. Christ's word is true and it is authentic, 'for on him the Father, God himself, has set his seal.' (Jn 6: 27) Christ saves us by repairing the brokenness of humanity from within. He accomplishes this by creating a new community in which unity and harmony are fostered and continuously regenerated in the ministry of word and sacrament. Christ unites the new people of God in himself for they all reach out to him in faith; and he, in drawing all things to himself, reconciles us to the Father as he breathes into the restored and recreated community of humanity, of which the Church is the manifestation, the family Spirit who animates and pervades the inner life of the Trinity. Christ's redemption saves the human family by effectively constructing a new environment wherein it becomes possible, once more, for concord to prevail in relationships.

The saving life, ministry, passion and exaltation of Jesus Christ unseals in the barrenness of our sinful milieu, the fountain of baptism. The outward action of baptismal pouring, cleansing and immersing signifies an effective interior transformation of the human person. Baptism unlocks the door to repentance and thus to the possibility of re-orientation of ourselves in the direction of the Father. Baptism places us within the community of faith and so is the passport from our state of exile and condition of alienation. We are re-formed as the children of God in name and in fact and, consequently, heirs by God's own act! Christ thus redeems the whole creation by creating a family of faith pervaded by the radically new ethos of love. Through the Church this ethic of charity can permeate humanity making it possible for salvation to become a reality for all without exception, for all those, even, who seek God with a sincere heart according to the lights of their own consciences (Eucharistic Prayer IV).

The Truth that Christ reveals is the antidote to the ancient lie by which we were tricked and enslaved through our free co-operation with a scheme cunningly calculated to send us back to the dust from whence we came and to quench the Divine spark within us in a tide of despair and fear. It was a project that the first human beings had given their assent to, God having created us with a vital element of free will so that we could truly exist in his image and likeness and have the potential to chose Love of our own accord. That very gift of freedom, however, was to be the 'Achilles heel' of humanity, the vulnerable spot struck by the crafty serpent who, in the story of the fall, epitomises the malevolent force of darkness and disorder.

But any serum or antidote, if it is to be effective, must actually enter in some shape or form, the body that is afflicted. The virus or infection must be tackled from within. And so it was that the Eternal Word who was with God in the beginning is made flesh and blood. This is the wonderful mystery of our salvation – the Word was made flesh, he lived among us. This sentence is one of the most sacred in scripture. It is like a small capsule containing an almighty expression of the love of God in action. The Word was made flesh; think of what this means. The Eternal Word – God speaking in eternity and his Word communicates life, love and light – the Eternal God who is always present in eternity and for eternity expresses himself in terms of life, love and light; and now, in time, he translates this Word into flesh so that our ears can perceive, our eyes see, and our hands touch, the Word who is life.

The Word was made flesh. Flesh. We use that term in different ways. We say of ourselves, for example: 'I'm only flesh and blood after all', to explain that we are only human and not super-men or wonder-women. The expression that St John uses, flesh, is the same term employed by St Paul to describe our frail, weak and fallen human nature. That the Word became flesh means that God has really become one of us – sharing our fragility, our bruisedness – the things that make us cry and make us laugh; the things that fill us with hope and fill us with fear. That the Word became flesh means that he was tempted in every way that we are, though he is without sin (Heb 4: 15-16), so that, with him, we could be delivered from sin and live holy and spotless through love in his presence; a purpose for which the Father chose us, in Christ, before the world was made (Eph 1: 3-5).

And there is another way in which we use the term flesh: we say of our nearest and dearest, 'he or she is my own flesh and blood.' We describe our family as flesh of our flesh and we declare that blood is thicker than water. And the Word who is God was made flesh and he lived among us. He becomes our very own. We can now address him as Abba, Daddy, because the Son is born our brother; and he fills us with the family Spirit of God: 'to all who did accept him he gave power to become children of God.' (Jn 1: 12) He lived among us – God – that literally translates from the Greek as he *pitched his tent*; or, in a more contemporary idiom, built his house among us. In other words he shares our lot. He accepts our fate. Our Creator becomes our neighbour; our Sovereign becomes our friend; the Holiest becomes our brother; the Almighty Lord becomes our companion; the Eternal God becomes our Abba – Father. God puts down roots among us. His Spirit, who comes to dwell in our midst, makes us one family; and in our family life together as the people of God, we discover what hope his call holds for us, what rich glories he has promised that we, the saints, will inherit.

He, Christ, is come so that, once more, we might have life to the full; so that, once again, the glory of God would be seen in our own flesh, that glory for which we are created and intended in the loving communion of the Trinity – our true home. This is what begins to unfold among us when Jesus the Christ was born the Son of Mary: God arrives in person to dress the wound and heal the division; to raise up what had fallen; to remove the sting of death and destroy its paralysing grip over humankind.

In the beginning, God breathed a breath of life into the nostrils of the first human person who thus became a living being (Gen 2:7). That kiss of life was the opening of many channels of communication. The picture we have from Genesis is that, before the Fall, man and woman enjoyed an intimacy with God; an almost homely atmosphere prevailed where, 'the sound of God could be heard walking in the garden in the cool of the day' (Gen 3:8). Creation itself is a means or medium whereby God broadcasts the reality of who he is and who we are. Human experience too, is a direct line of inter-action between God and humanity. Man and woman are, after all, in the image and likeness of God; and so, naturally, God would choose human beings to begin the unfolding of his purpose and plan, in successive generations. Therefore, it was the weak and trembling hands of mortal flesh that began to lift 'the mourning veil covering all people and the shroud enwrapping all nations', the final removal of which would fill the world with the splendour of undying light when, in Christ, the rising sun would at last visit us like the dawn from on high (Lk 1:78).

This began to be accomplished in the actions of patriarchs and by the words of prophets. Through Abraham and then Moses, God began to prepare humanity to realise its destiny – a destiny obscured, when God's image and likeness in the human person, was distorted by the first sin. The chain reaction of sin set in motion at the fall caused humanity to fall out of relationship with God and into a self-imposed exile of alienation. However, even when humanity found itself disfigured and wandering in the wilderness of estrangement, God did not abandon us to our inevitable ruin. Had he turned away from us, we would have surely been lost: but instead, because Love is his name, he set in motion his wondrous plan of salvation – the means whereby, we would be recovered, reconciled and restored.

God laid the foundations of his mighty redemptive act, by calling together a single nation, Israel. At the outset of humanity's pilgrimage of faith homeward, God swore an oath to Abraham when he said: 'Leave your country, your family, and your father's house for the land I will show you. I will make you a great nation. I will bless you and make your name so famous that it will be used as a blessing' (Gen 12:1-2).

God's call to Abraham was a challenge to cash in every last penny of his comfort, certainty and security and to invest his own life and the future of his children and descendants in God alone. A promise is then made by God upon receipt of Abraham's trusting pledge of faith; a promise of blessing undreamt of; a promise kept when there was born for us a Saviour who is Christ the Lord (Lk 2:11). In him is the fullness of life and every blessing.

Before the dawning of that endless day, however, Israel would serve as the vehicle through which God would gather all the nations to himself and through which all the ends of the earth would eventually see the salvation of God. Through the words of prophets, he patiently and sometimes less than patiently, directed the wayward and stumbling steps, of his stiff-necked and headstrong people. Again and again he reasoned with them, cajoled and threatened, chastised when necessary, but then once again rushing to their side to console and rebuild them out of the ruins of their own self-destruction, never giving up on this people on whom he had set his heart.

The Old Testament scriptures speak to us of our origins and do more than hint of a glorious destiny. Indeed they are pregnant with the promise of one who is to come, he who is to be sent to us, he, the hope of the nations (Gen 49:10). Since humanity's betrayal of God and itself at the fall, the eyes of many prophets and holy people scanned the horizon of time watching and waiting, longing and yearning. The pleading hope of so many is well expressed in Isaiah 64:1-2:

> Oh that you would tear the heavens open and come down – at your presence the mountains would melt …

One was sought who would cause the wilderness of alienation to bloom once more and rejoice at the sound of God's step drawing near; one was yearned for, who would demolish the mountains of separation; he was awaited, who would save his people from their sins and walk them homewards.

I will leave this place and go to my Father
Blessed, therefore, are our eyes because they see, our ears because they hear. For truly, says Christ, many prophets and holy people longed to hear what you hear and never heard it, to see what you see and never saw it. For now '… we do see in Jesus one who was for a short while made lower than the angels and is now crowned with glory and splendour because he submitted to death; by God's grace he had to experience death for all' (Heb 2:9). For now, 'Christ has come, as the high priest of all the blessings which were to come' (Heb 9:11). Our eyes have at last seen unveiled, the salvation which God has made ready, in the sight of all the nations (Lk 2:29-32). Our ears are astonished at the gracious words that come from the lips of him who proclaims the glorious gospel of death abolished, and life, in its fullness, restored (*cf* Lk 4:18-22, 2 Tim 1:10). Abraham's faith is justified and his trustful hope fulfilled, beyond anyone's wildest imaginings.

Christ is born our brother in the flesh. He takes his stand at our side and begins to persuade us out of our shadow land. His words and actions speak of recovery, healing, restoration and renovation. He declares: 'I have come so that they may have life to the full' (Jn 10:10). Christ's credentials are presented by John at the end of the prologue to his gospel, when he says: 'No-one has ever seen God; it is the only Son, who is nearest to the Father's heart, who has made him known (Jn 1:18).

Christ is thus infinitely qualified to reveal the Father and makes it known that the heart of God is like that of any parent, who loves or who has ever lost a wayward son or daughter. God is like a Father who allows his son the freedom to make choices, even to make mistakes, yet who watches, sentry-like, for his return. The gospel parable referred to, Luke 15:11-32, tell us that the father saw the boy coming from a long way off and ran to meet him. He must, therefore, like so many a parent, have been watching out or waiting up, eyes fixed often on the distant hills, 'Perhaps he will come today. Ah well, maybe tomorrow after all.' How many mothers and fathers know well that scenario; not closing their eyes perhaps, until they hear the sound of the latch and the door close as the last one comes in for the night. Even though the 'child' they await, is twenty- or thirty-something.

When the Father meets the boy, there are no rebukes or lectures, no matter how well-deserved in this case. He runs to his son, clasps him in his arms and kisses him – then there is a party, a grand celebration to welcome the stray home in true style! All, however, is not as it should be just yet. As we have seen, the first casualties of sin were compassion and communion. The elder brother refuses to rejoice and stays aloof from the family celebration. It means nothing to him that his brother was dead and has come back to life. He, after all, brought it all on himself and as such deserves all he got. Such narrow-minded vindictiveness is the enemy of salvation. It is a refusal to come in out of the cold and to acknowledge ones family. The mission of Christ is to re-establish communion and teach us compassion for one another. For we are all children of the one Father and, as such, sisters and brothers of one another.

God, in his Son, was intent on giving expression to the depth of his fervent love for human beings. Yet much of the playing hard to get, or downright refusal to be wooed at all, that God encounters in humanity, wears a mask of pseudo-religosity. Like the elder

brother, who had kept all the rules, there are those who feel that
the sinner should get all that is coming to him. Such an attitude refuses to make room at the table, refuses to celebrate and to share
and, as such, is the antithesis of genuine religion. Jesus encountered much hostility and opposition from those of this mindset.
Those who come to his side however, are liberated from the com-
pulsion towards self-preservation. They are free to celebrate in
thanksgiving the tender compassion and the embrace of God
which they receive in Christ. The gospel of Christ always reminds
us of the love that is expected of us. We are accountable for what
God has invested in us – the life we have received from him. For it
is only those who learn to forget themselves in love for others,
who can ever know the real meaning of life and the hidden significance of every single human being. That is the life we all share as
his uniquely beloved children. In Christ, we are all related to God
and to one another. Because of the close family ties established
therefore, Christ can say: 'I tell you solemnly, in so far as you did
this to one of the least of these sisters and brothers of mine, you
did it to me' (Mt 25:40).

Jesus Christ: God in solidarity with us
The real and living God is far from 'stand-offish'. We learn in
Christ his enthusiasm for us and his desire to be near us. Some,
however, might ask: 'Is he a fair weather God? Is he willing to, in
a sense, put his money where is mouth is, and stand with us even
in the line of fire?' The age old case in point is this: when human
beings find themselves caught in the crucible of suffering, where
is God then? And what does he have to say?

The expanse of human experience touched by pain and anguish,
is the vast and lonely place where God's presence is most often
called into question. Does God have a case to answer? Humanity,
in its dilemma, has the right to ask the questions and weigh up the
facts. Particularly as we continue to hear the universal cry of distress that goes up, day and night, across the earth; the groans of
those unjustly imprisoned and brutally treated; the cries of those
who lack food and other basic necessities for human life with dignity; the laments of all the contemporary Rachels who weep for
their children who are no more; the tears of all who, in whatever
capacity, suffer pain and hurt for no apparent reason or justifica-

tion. Where is God to be seen through all this mist of tears? What gracious words does he offer in this dark place? And so, there is a sense in which we put God on trial. In doing so, we owe him the obligation of a fair hearing and a decision based on the facts. What part does God play in the drama of human sorrow and what explanation does he offer? Let us take the evidence of the prophet:

> Without beauty, without majesty we saw him, no looks to attract our eyes; a thing despised and rejected by men, a man of sorrows and familiar with suffering, a man to make people screen their faces; he was despised and we took no account of him. And yet ours were the suffering he bore, ours the sorrows he carried (Is 53:2-3).

That man before Pilate, falsely accused and condemned unjustly; this man who was stripped, tortured, spat upon, kicked and beaten by soldiers; that person being ridiculed, insulted, flogged and crowned with thorns – Behold your God. Behold the Man. Where is your God? Here he is! That body disfigured, broken, lifeless and cold upon the cross, is the human body of the Word made flesh, the word who speaks life, love and hope. That Word addressed to us by the Father, calling us into existence and abundant life. Look and see. Do the facts not speak for themselves? Does he not walk with us every step of the painful way? Even when the road leads to darkness and tears? Not only is God acquitted with no case to answer, he has opened a way out for us, from that ravine as dark as death. He has provided the means, by his own suffering and death, whereby it is possible to climb out of the abyss of fear and despair.

When we regard this bloodstained and dead figure, we are face to face with the ultimate gesture of solidarity on God's behalf. God is truly with us! Especially when we too are in agony; even when we ourselves must stand in the face of death. He comes to our side, not because he is answerable for, or in any way culpable in regard to our plight, but simply because we are loved by him. That is why he takes his place beside us. Where, therefore, is God amidst all the world's pain and humanity's sorrow? He is here! He is at the centre of each breaking heart and looking out of every eye that is red from weeping. He stands with them, for it is he who is a victim with them and for them.

The fact about much of our human suffering is that it is either self-inflicted or the result, directly or indirectly, of the selfishness, greed and indifference of the other members of the human race. There is also, however, that bewildering form of tragedy which comes out of the blue, like a mindless cyclone of pain, and churns up incredulous grief from the families and peoples upon whom it falls. There are, for example, the great evils of natural disaster, freak accidents, meaningless catastrophes, sudden death and illness for which there seems to be no coherent cause or logical explanation. There would appear to be at large, within wounded and broken creation, a virulent spasm of agony which grips and befalls the human family seemingly at random, a swirling mass of evil which can visit both individuals and nations and for which there is no justification. There are many situations of sorrow in human experience which defy explanation. There are many people whose pain is too profound to bear philosophising or any kind of verbalising. Faith does not anaesthetise anyone to this reality, neither does it dare to offer glib platitudes. We hear only the assurance, 'I am with you.' In the midst of the created order, which groans and cries out in its woundedness, we remember the words of God among us, 'this sickness will not end in death but in God's glory ...' (Jn 11:4). For creation itself retains the hope of being freed, like us, from its slavery to decadence, and its groaning is, in fact, one great act of giving birth to the New Creation (cf Rom 8:21-24).

Christ is the one who stoops from the heights to look down on heaven and earth (Ps 113:4-6). He is God's hand extended to raise the poor from the dust and the needy from the dung-hill, to give them a place among princes (Ps 113:68). Is this not exactly what the Father did for his wayward son when, after coming to his senses, he made his way home expecting a rebuke and the lowest place? For although, 'we all had gone astray like sheep, each taking his own way', God in Christ cancelled every record of the debt we had to pay, he did away with it by nailing it to the cross (Is 53:6, Col 2:14).

God's response to the reality of pain and the consequences of injustice for the powerless, is one of actions speaking louder than words. It is the reaction of a parent, for the mother and father of an ailing child, share uniquely in that suffering. God answers our helpless and bewildered 'Why?' by entering completely, in utter compassion, into the sheer agony of the crushed, the condemned, the tormented and the despairing; he replies to our predicament by suffering with us himself. In his so doing, however, the reality that gives rise to cries and sighs does not appear to be altered. Yet it is a matter of the most profound consequence and crucial significance that God, in Christ, has allowed himself to be cruelly treated, brutalised and murdered. For in doing so, he has initiated the escape route from absurdity and despair. Christ, in his passion and death, has gone into the very heart of darkness and dealt there, face to face, with the horrendous monstrosity of evil. He has gone to the source of the malaise that fills the human heart with such foreboding and dread. He engages the problem of suffering from within. He confounds it, not by removing it, but by filling even that horrific place with the reality of who he is! For he is life itself.

> Life that was the light of men; and light shines in the darkness, and darkness could not overpower it (Jn 1:5).

In his being killed, Christ enters that ravine as dark as death (Ps 23:4), plumbing its fathomless depths; those deep places of blackness that seek to drown the human spirit in nothingness. In dying, the Word, who was with God in the beginning, speaks in that fearful place. There, in the midst of death, is spoken the Word through whom all things come to be (Jn 1:1-3). God says, in Christ, let there be life where there is only death; and the formless void, the emptiness of death, that final frontier of darkness, is suffused with the light of his being there. Death's shadowy regions dissipate before him who is life and love, light and hope. The infinite force of the love of God is unleashed in the domain of death, and the evil one's plan for the ruination of humanity is forever thwarted.

When the mortal body of Christ lies cold and lifeless in the tomb, the Spirit of his love acts upon death, rendering it impotent, null and void. Having fulfilled the work the Father gave him to do, the mighty conqueror reappears, having established forever the situation, whereby those who listen to his voice and keep his word will never see death, will never be lost or stolen from his hand (Jn

8:51, 10:28). Death has no power over him anymore; its kingdom lies in ruins, around the feet of Christ risen and glorified. Forever more the community of faith will rejoice and sing:

> O happy fault, O necessary sin of Adam, which gained for us so great a Redeemer!

Humanity that had been banished is now free to come home for God himself has found us; and the cherubs with their swords of flashing fire (Gen 3:24) are relieved of their post. God has embraced us in the dark and now reveals himself in the new language of death that leads to resurrection. He speaks to us now, face to face, in his Son, in terms of bitter wood moistened by the tears of him who, during his life on earth, offered up prayer and entreaty to the one who had the power to save him out of death (Heb 5:7-10), and moistened with his own life's blood, until it is changed, by his love, into the tree of life. Having been welcomed home by Christ, the Father lifts us up with his Son, so that we can freely pluck the fruit of that tree – the food of life – the wheat and the grapes which are brimming with the utter fullness of God.

CHAPTER THREE

Discipleship: Life from a cross and resurrection perspective

The language of the cross: a Word addressed to the heart
God addresses himself to the heart of every individual, whatever their state in life, in the language of the cross. There are several dialects in his basic mode of communication, each one designed to be understood according to the milieu of the one who hears it: priests and consecrated religious will interpret its demands in the light of the radical challenge to live out discipleship, peculiar to and implicit in, their specific vocation; those called to Christian marriage will find the same voice of Christ addressing them as they commit themselves to each other for better, for worse, for richer, for poorer, in sickness and in health all the days of their lives.

God speaks to the hearts of all the baptised: priests, religious, married and single. His Word is deciphered as a dying to self which contains the seed of new and limitless Life. In the mystery of our baptism, and our constant sharing in the life of Jesus Christ through his paschal sacrifice, our living and dying is reformulated according to the grammar by which God expresses himself as endless Love and eternal Life, which he intends to share with us. The route of our earthly journey from birth – through life – to death – is reoriented towards our true home, the new and eternal Jerusalem, that everlasting space made holy by the presence of the Trinity.

The language of the cross is addressed to the heart of a human being, to the inner self of a person. Thus it is that they appear illogical and apparently foolish when we attempt a critique of them in the light of ordinary human reasoning. It is only in the light of God's all-consuming Love for us that such words as these spoken by Christ can be interpreted:

Anyone who comes to me without hating father, mother, wife,

children, brothers, sisters, yes and their own life too, cannot be
my disciple ... None of you can be my disciple without giving
up all you own. (Lk 14: 25-27.33)

Such words, on the surface, would seem to go against the grain of
our existence as flesh and blood mortals with needs and require-
ments. You must abandon all – possessions, relationships, stabili-
ty, comfort – yes, and your own life too. How are we to translate
this call in an appropriate mode for our manner of living? Such a
demand seems, at first reading, altogether too much. Small wonder, we might think, that people actually take fright and take
flight from such a God. We need, however, to bear in mind the
context in which God speaks these words, and interpret them
according to what is appropriate for our life style. The manner in
which religious apply this call of Christ to their lives will differ
radically from a married woman or man.

There are, as St Paul reminds us, all sorts of gifts and services to be
done but always for the same Lord in the one Spirit. (cf. 1 Cor 12:
1) There are all kinds of modes of discipleship and each of us has
been given his or her own share of grace (Eph 4: 7). Married people are called to give up all things in the vocation of loving one another and their families. Such is the essence of healthy married life
and love. Detachment is certainly advisable when we consider
what possessiveness and pre-occupation with material comforts
can do to married and family life. Detachment frees us from that
obsessive and unhealthy attachment which can kill love between
spouses, friends and even parent and child.

The love of God relentlessly pursues the human heart. It is a passionate love and it confronts us persistently, in spite of our efforts
to dodge the issues it faces with us. In many respects it is the Love
that revealed itself in terms of the prophet Hosea's forsaken husband. Israel, God's beloved people, are likened to a faithless and
adulterous wife who, having forsaken her true husband and first
love, has played the harlot with many and disgraced herself utterly.

This is why I shall block her way with thorns, and wall her in to
stop her in her tracks; then if she chases her lovers she will not
catch them, if she looks for them she will not find them, and

then she will say, 'I shall go back to my first husband, I was better off then than I am now' (Hosea 2: 8-10).

The amazing thing about the love of God, as described by Hosea, is its long suffering patience and willingness to forgive; for in spite of the wife's breach of trust and the ostensibly selfish reasons for her going back to him, the husband is actually plotting as to how he will rekindle and reclaim this love, which, to all intents and purposes, is so fickle as to be undeserving of trust and unworthy of a second chance. Thus does God use the language of a lover besotted, in order to seduce the human heart. Such is the way he allures us into the desert of detachment so as to speak to our hearts undisturbed and free from distraction.

Why, however, is God so uncompromising in his demands? What does he mean when he asks that we give up all that we own? What are the implications of such a daunting challenge for my life as a married, single or celibate follower of Jesus Christ? What does detachment mean for the average disciple who walks, not in a cloister, but in the busy environment of commitments at home, at work, and in society generally?

I am called to speak the language of the cross of Christ in whatever situation my life places me in. What, after all, is a mother or father doing in caring for their children and one another if not offering themselves, in a very radical manner, for the life of those entrusted to their care? Their daily sacrifices take place usually at the unadorned altars of kitchen table, washing machines and sinks. The rituals associated with their offering are normally undramatic and usually unnoticed, and its rubric involves much of the following: early rising, struggling to make ends meet, efforts to put food on the table and clothes on the back, sometimes sleepless nights, hours of work and little recreation.

All of this, and more, is the 'nitty gritty' of responding wholeheartedly to the vocation of Christian married life. For so many today, the heroic sacrifice of men and women in married and family life, is accentuated by the martyrdom of unemployment with its attendant assaults on human dignity and integrity. There are many Christian disciples, husbands and wives, mothers and father, married and un-married, young, middle-aged and older, who give undaunted witness to the values of the Gospel which are implicitly affirmative of our humanity, in the midst of situations and while faced with elements that are corrosive of it.

In the parish of the Nativity, Poleglass, where I am presently a curate, 75-80% of men are without work. Such massive unemployment can create a fairly bleak and soulless landscape. However, there are many ordinary people who have not allowed their victimisation to shape or dictate their identity. Sadly, there are those who have, and we are indeed dogged by all the social ills and afflictions that can stem from poverty. Yet, the many enterprising schemes and initiatives taken at local level to create employment, shopping and leisure facilities – much of it animated by the concern and enthusiasm of the parish priest, Patrick McWilliams – would indicate clearly that it is possible to carry one's cross after Jesus Christ with positive courage and creative results, causing the wilderness of dried-up lives and lands to rejoice, to bloom and to produce fruit. Yes, it is possible to interpret our apparent hopelessness and make new sense of it, when we employ the grammar and vocabulary which Jesus Christ reveals to those who accompany him.

Christian discipleship, whether one be an ordained, religious or lay person, is a matter of learning the language of the cross which for many is folly and an obstacle they cannot get over (cf. 1 Cor 17-25). The disciple is a student of the apparent foolishness of God; the believer is one whose eye is trained to see beyond the supposed madness of the cross and so to recognise how, in God's plan and by his action, what would have been the downfall of humanity, a bottomless pit of despair and abandonment, has been transformed from within by the Risen Christ. For Christ has rewritten our human story and transposed our lamentable defeat into the canticle of our Passover triumph over death, with him. The cross – that tree of bitter death and barren wood – becomes the vehicle whereby eternal blessings arrive. The cross becomes the doorway to the realisation of our full stature and potential in the fullness of life made ready for us.

The cross is the strong arm of God, his mighty hand outstretched to take hold of us and rescue us from darkness, emptiness, and the absurdity of a life lived without rhyme or reason; a life which is become a vacuum of despair; a life where we are nothing more than slaves at the beck and call of cravings, instincts and desires; a life in which we are, finally and completely, swallowed up by death. Humanity, by its very nature, rebels and cries out against such a fate. God, in his Son who comes among us, hears that cry and steers us into a new Exodus journey, which leads to the new heavens and the new earth.

The way of the cross will arrive at a day when the joy of the Resurrection will renew the whole world (cf. Prefaces of Easter I-V); a day on which we will find God and he will clasp us in his arms, causing us to be transfigured by his sheer delight in us. With tender hand he will caress our wounded hearts and wipe away our tears (cf. Isaiah 25:8). He will dress us in the best robe, put a ring on our finger and sandals on our feet (cf. Lk 15:22). His face will be radiant with joy at the sight of us. His love will wash us and make us new so that, once more, we shall be like him; for we shall see him as he really is (cf. 1 Jn 3:2). That day will see the beginning of such songs as will never end!

> The language of the Cross may be illogical to those who are not on the way to salvation, but those of us who are on the way see it as God's power to save ... and so, here are we preaching a crucified Christ; to (some) an obstacle they cannot get over, to (others) madness, but to those who have been called (no matter who they may be), a Christ who is the wisdom and power of God. For God's foolishness is wiser than human wisdom and God's weakness is stronger than human strength (1 Cor 1:22-25).

Our faith is intelligible only from the vantage point of a Calvary bathed in Easter morning sunlight. The language of the cross, in all its different dialects, articulates love which is stronger than death. To learn this truth we must cease to live merely on the surface of life but allow the Spirit to lead us into its depths. For it is there, at the core of reality, that we meet Christ who has crushed and defeated the power of evil. It was no cosmetic exercise he was engaged in but a going into the heart of darkness, a descent into all the hellish scenarios that paralyse and oppress women and men.

And having dealt there with the cause of our distress, he takes captivity captive, bestowing the gifts that raise us up, with him, to the highest heights of glory (cf. Eph 4: 8-13). For the glory of God is man and woman fully alive! (St Irenaeus) He makes us fully alive and free indeed! In his company, we are enabled to live already, even in a broken, imperfect and bruised world, as hope-filled people who make Love present by a manner of acting and in a mode of living that springs from a living faith, until we become fully mature with the fullness of Christ himself (Eph 4:13).

Detachment: the positive use of our exile
If we are to rise with him to the heights for which we are destined, however, there will have to be a certain amount of shaking off and shedding that excess baggage that keeps us too much on the earth. St Paul advises:

> Since you have been brought back to true life with Christ, you must look for the things that are in heaven, where Christ is, sitting a God's right hand. Let your thoughts be on heavenly things, not on the things that are on the earth, because you have died, and now the life you have is hidden with Christ in God. But when Christ is revealed – and he is your life– you too will be revealed in all your glory with him (Col 3: 1-4).

We might get worried, however, on hearing this mention of having our thoughts only on heavenly things. What of those old charges about being so heavenly minded as to be of no earthly use? How am I expected to live according to Paul's ideal when I have a house and a family to organise? A school or business to run? A busy and demanding parish to care for and administer? Is it possible, and indeed practical, with all the concerns of growing up and growing old, to look only for the things that are in heaven? Notice that St Paul speaks of our having been brought back to *true life* with Christ. The spiritual life of a Christian is to develop that true life and to integrate it with our earthly lives, here and how, so that there is no dichotomy, contradiction or compartmentalisation between one and the other. The life that we receive from God, both spiritually and bodily, is symmetrically symphonic and stems from the same source. The true life of the Spirit that the Risen Christ breathed on us at our baptism, is inextricably woven into the substance of our bodily existence, so much so, that the apostle writes in another place:

> We know that when the tent we live in on earth (i.e. the body) is folded up, there is a house built by God for us, an everlasting home not made by human hands, in the heavens. We are always full of confidence, then, when we remember that to live in the body means to be exiled from the Lord, going as we do by faith and not by sight – we are full of confidence, I say, and actually want to be exiled from the body and make our home with the Lord. Whether we are living in the body or exiled from it, we are intent on pleasing him. For all the truth about us will be brought out in the law court of Christ, and each of us will get what we deserve for the things we did in the body, good or bad (2 Cor 5: 1-2, 6-10).

Our earthly existence, already contains the substance of eternal life, because we are joined to Jesus Christ at baptism, and that living link is nurtured and sustained through the Eucharist and other sacraments. I don't think therefore, that it would be an exaggeration to say that our lives in this world are a matter of using our present exile from the Lord in the most positive and effective manner that we can. The essence of Divine life present within us, is shown forth in the actualisation of our Christian vocation as parents, priests, teachers, married or single, consecrated religious, laity, or whatever walk of life God's providence has placed us in.

At the core of our discipleship, our companionship with Christ, is our Lord's invitation to take up our cross and follow him; his call to give up all that we own. This is not as impractical as we might at first suspect. Genuine love embraces detachment quite enthusiastically and happily. Here is a practical example of what detachment means. When a person falls in love there is a radical forgetting of oneself involved, as the object of our affections becomes the focus of our thoughts and emotions. The person loved becomes the context in which we decide our priorities and set our agenda. Decisions and even alterations to our lifestyle are freely and joyfully made, in order to create the necessary time and the conditions favourable to a healthy development of relationship and friendship with the one who is loved.

Detachment is also the essence of Christian married love. En-gaged couples and husbands and wives are required to put them-selves out for one another. It is no longer possible to live the life-style of single persons; there is a very practical forgetfulness of self involved that must be mutual and balanced. In embracing Christian marriage one has, hopefully, decided to detach oneself from the former lifestyle of being 'young, free and single'. In the Sacrament of Marriage 'they become one body'. One's priorities are therefore radically altered.

Detachment is also the flavour of parental and filial love: mothers and fathers, when they co-operate with the Creator Father in bringing a child into the world, are also bestowing a further sacri-ficial character on their life together. Parents must constantly make sacrifices for their children to feed, clothe, educate and rear them with decency. This would be impossible were they attached to their own comforts and interests. The unsung heroic generosity of parents should then invite the children to embrace and recipro-cate this manner of loving, in their relating to their parents and those around them. It is such an ethos of unselfish and generous love that the Christian family, in partnership with the parish school, seeks to impart.

When a newly ordained priest is presented with bread and wine by the bishop for his first celebration of the Eucharistic sacrifice, the bishop addresses him as follows: 'Accept from the holy people of God the gifts to be offered to him. Know what you are doing, and imitate the mystery you celebrate: model your life on the mystery of the Lord's cross.'

There is sufficient fruit in these two short sentences for a lifetime's contemplation. The life of a priest is characterised by the offering of sacrifice expressed, above all, at the altar each day; it is articu-lated in his constant prayer for the Church, the world and the peo-ple entrusted to his care; it is borne witness to in his celibacy for the sake of the kingdom; and is concretised in his pastoral minis-try among the faithful. The brand of detachment peculiar to the priesthood is coloured and given nuance in the giving of one's life in the service of God and for the salvation of his people, whilst striving to grow in the likeness of Christ and honouring God by a courageous witness of faith and love (cf. Preface of Priesthood, *Roman Missal*).

The priesthood is a call to allow the Word spoken each day at Mass to become flesh among the people of God in our whole-hearted service of them: 'This is my Body which will be given up for you. This is the cup of my Blood ... It will be shed for you and for all so that sins may be forgiven.' The entire mystery of God among us – the Incarnate Word – is the effecting of reconciliation and the forgiveness of sins. This reality is perpetuated in the priestly apostolate as expressed by St Paul:

> From now onwards, therefore, we do not judge anyone by the standards of the flesh. Even if we did once know Christ in the flesh, that is not how we know him now. And for anyone who is in Christ, there is a new creation; the old creation has gone, and now the new one is here. It is all God's work. It was God who reconciled us to himself through Christ and gave us the work of handing on this reconciliation ... he has entrusted to us the news that they are reconciled. So we are ambassadors for Christ; it is as though God were appealing through us, and the appeal that we make in Christ's name is: be reconciled to God (2 Cor 5: 16-20).

The Eucharist, which is at the very centre of a priest's life and which is the fount and summit of the lives of all disciples, is the re-presentation of the Lord's sacrifice by which he restores unity to all creation and to the fragmented family of humanity. This wondrous mystery of the Incarnate Word – God drawing near to us – is well expressed in Christmas Preface III: '*Today in him a new light has dawned upon the world: God has become one again with man and man has become one again with God. Your eternal Word has taken upon himself our human weakness, giving our mortal nature immortal value. so marvellous is this oneness between God and man that in Christ man restores to man the gift of everlasting life.* '

This marvellous oneness is highlighted even further in the mystery of our being made one body, one spirit in Christ through our sacramental grafting onto him. In this manner the Word is made flesh in us: in the lives of priests who offer themselves to God for the service of his people; in the lives of religious men and women whose poverty, chastity and obedience indicate the transitory nature of this earthly life and the coming kingdom which will have no end; in the lives of wives and husbands, mothers and fathers who give of themselves for each other and for their children, at the domestic altar of hearth and home, and in the work-place; in Catholic teachers as they labour at the task of educating and inculcating the ethos of the Gospel; and in all those, of whatever age or station, who make Christ present in a life of faith and waiting in joyful hope, revealed in prayer and acts of love.

Detachment should not frighten us so much when we consider it as something that many people already do out of love, and out of necessity for their chosen way of living. Detachment is basically the loosening of those bonds which tie us to selfish interest and self-seeking; it is a process of freeing ourselves for genuine love which always has the interest of the other(s) at heart. The positive response to our Lord's invitation to leave all and take up our cross each day and follow him, is expressed just as validly and effectively in the active apostolate of Christian witness and ministry in the world, as it is in the contemplative life of the cloistered religious. For detachment is the art of keeping all things in their correct focus. When either persons or things get out of perspective in our lives, then the real issues of our true life become clouded, and havoc is wreaked with our contentment, happiness and peace of soul. We lose our way and are unable to find God whom we can approach only in poverty of spirit.

In this world we can only have faint inklings of the glory for which we are created – the welcome God has prepared for those who love him. That glory being kept for us in the heavens will result in our total fulfilment and our being perfected as human beings. God desires therefore, to give us everything – to give us himself! He created us for himself: that is why we discover in ourselves a desire for nothing less than everything; a hunger and a thirst that is never satiated; a constant searching for something that we cannot quite put our finger on. We are created as 'all or nothing' persons. The great tragedy is when we attempt to fulfil our deepest yearnings with things which can never ultimately satisfy or remotely produce the bread we seek. To spare us this misery and fruitless heartaches, Jesus advises us:

> Do not work for food that cannot last, but work for food that endures to eternal life, the kind of food the Son of Man is offering you, for on him the Father, God himself, has set his seal (Jn 6: 27).

He goes on to describe himself to his listeners as the true bread they are seeking: 'I am the Bread of Life. Whoever comes to me will never be hungry; whoever believes in me will never thirst.' When we come to him we are already working for the food that endures to eternal life. Our lives are given new significance. All the favours and services that we render to one another become intimately associated with Christ's doing of the Father's will, for he goes on to say, in regard to his gift of the Eucharist: 'Whoever eats my flesh and drinks my blood lives in me an I live in them. As I, who am sent by the living Father, myself draw life from the Father, so whoever eats me will draw life from me' (Jn 6: 56-57).

It is necessary, whatever one's state in life, to ensure that the eyes of faith are properly adjusted and focused, in order to keep the Lord ever in our sight; in order to ensure that we draw life from him. Detachment is a process initiated by our coming to him empty handed and unshackled. It is part of our progress and development towards him, which he lovingly and gently oversees and navigates. The invitation to do the will of God in the vineyard of this earthly life, is a challenge to work off our excess weight, to cast aside all the unnecessary things that hold us back, that complicate the issue of our loving, that prevent us from living wholesome and joyous lives of generosity, in loving and serving God and one another. The spiritual doctrine of detachment frees us to truly love and be loved; it guards us against addiction to things and even to persons.

True love is liberating and non-possessive. Detachment, however, does not mean a cold aloofness in our relationships, but implies a manner of loving that tries to be free of any hidden agenda of self-interest: detachment fosters a love that is empowering; a love that doesn't smother, but which encourages the other to be fully his or her self. Very often this is the painful lesson in love that parents learn as they watch their children grow up and 'fly the nest'. It is a painful love but necessary for the good of the child who is loved. Likewise, the love of God for us is intensely fervent and indeed passionate, but it never stifles or obliterates us. It enhances, cherishes and helps us reach our full stature and potential in him. Christian love, in its marital, chaste or celibate expression, must always try to mirror that Divine love. Non-possessive, detached loving will never seek to exploit or to subtly manipulate others to get its own way, but will strive always to make them feel valued and respected; and to be a life-giving and freeing affirmation of those around us.

A rich person has no need of anything; they have all they need and more. That is why God, in calling us to discipleship, asks us to be poor in spirit, that he might enrich us himself with treasure that endures. True and lasting riches, these are the delights he will reward us with in the kingdom, if we are generous and courageous enough to spend ourselves in his vineyard – the place in which I have been placed by him – my home, neighbourhood and parish. These localities are the holy ground where he is really present and where he awaits us in the people that we encounter there.

The goal of our faith-journey is nothing less than God himself; to see him as he really is; to possess him and be possessed by him. In asking us to free ourselves from all unhealthy attachments, he is preparing us to be attached to him for ever and to be filled with his utter fullness. It is his power at work in us, making our hidden selves to grow strong, that can do infinitely more that we can ask or imagine. Glory be to him! (cf. Eph 3: 14-21) Such is the prize for which Christ Jesus captured us, taking hold of us from the arms of the cross, that he might bring us with him towards the Resurrection and into the New Creation (cf. Phil 3:8-14).

The logic of the cross of Christ

Christ teaches his disciples to reason according to the new law of love that is promulgated in his death and resurrection. For it is the apparent foolishness of God, the enormity of his love revealed in the helpless vulnerability of Jesus Christ, the all-powerful Word made flesh, that saves the world. Let us consider the case of where Christ says to us: 'Love your enemies, pray for those who persecute you...' (Mt 5: 43045) Does he realise just how much he is asking? For some, these words prove all too difficult to accept; even for people with a genuine concern for what is right and a sincere desire to see an end to oppression and injustice. How, they ask, can we be expected to love those who trample upon us? How can we pray for and offer no resistance to those who would deprive us of life itself? This is surely too much even for God to ask. Love your enemies; pray for those who persecute you; offer the wicked no resistance. In calling us to act thus, is God asking us to confront a monster with a paper sword?

Hatred is indeed a veritable monstrosity; and, in our own time, it continues to stalk the earth, leaving in its wake the debris of broken families, communities and nations. The monster thrives best in an environment where hearts are hard with the thought of past hurts; where the possibility of forgiveness and charity is inhospitably received by remembered injustices. Hatred finds a conducive habitat in hearts that nurse grievances and nurture bitterness. The monster of hate is an irrational creature of uncontrollable fury. There is only one way for it to be over-powered, contained and prevented from venting it's destructive spleen on humanity, and to discover it we must listen to the reasoning of Christ.

Christ has equipped us with the truth about ourselves and about our human situation. St Paul forcefully reminds us of it: 'Didn't you realise that you were God's temple and that the Spirit of God was living among you? If anybody should destroy the temple of God, God will destroy them, because the temple of God is sacred; and you are that temple!' (1 Cor 3: 15-17)

It is in Christ's words that we find the key to our salvation as a human family, for they uphold the equal dignity and value of every person and enshrine the sanctity of human life. It is, however, his actions above all else which turn that key, enabling us to escape, if we will, from the dark pit dug deep in our history by the blows and cuts of generations of internecine warring, strife and cruelty. We look at what Christ did himself when confronted with the awful realities of violent hate and contemptuous brutality. We look at what is did to him. We see him bloodied, tortured and dead. We see him like a thing thrown away (Ps 31: 12).

Psalm 31 is described as a prayer in time of ordeal and it can be interpreted as referring to Christ in the midst of his passion. Yet note the way the tormented sufferer cheers up at the remembrance of the marvels of love the Lord performs for him: *'But I put my trust in you, Lord, I say, "you are my God". My days are in your hands, rescue me from the hands of my enemies and persecutors; let your face smile on your servant, save me in your love ... Lord, how great your goodness, reserved for those who fear you, bestowed on those who take shelter in you, for all to see! Blessed be the Lord, who performs marvels of love for me (in a fortified city!) In my alarm I exclaimed, "I have been snatched out of your sight!" Yet you heard my petition when I called to you for help ... Be strong, let your heart be bold, all you who hope in the Lord!'* (Ps 31: 14-16. 19. 21-22. 24)

To love our enemies is to approach them with confidence in him who assures us thus: 'Do not be afraid of those who kill the body but cannot kill the soul; fear him rather who can destroy both body and soul in hell' (Mt 10: 28-29). The battle with our fear is perhaps the greatest one of all. Once fear has been mastered there is no stopping us. Our experience of the God who dwells within us should teach that there is indeed no need to be afraid. For the Spirit of him who raised Jesus from the dead is living in us also. And that being the case, then he who raised Jesus from the dead will give life to our own mortal bodies also, through his Spirit living and praying in us (cf. Rom 8:11. 26-27). Yes, he is with us, that Spirit who prayed in the depths of Jesus' being as he hung upon the cross:

My God, my God, why have you forsaken me? I call all day, my God, but you never answer, all night long I call and cannot rest... I am like water draining away, my bones are all disjointed, my heart is like wax, melting inside me;my palate is drier than a potsherd and my tongue is stuck to my jaw. A pack of dogs surrounds me, a gang of villains closed me in; they tie me hand and foot and leave me lying in the dust of death (Ps 22: 1-2. 14-15d).

How well do we know that sensation of being stricken and not sure of where or to whom to go for help? The words of Psalm 22 are formulated by the Holy Spirit out of the depths of human anguish and that great sorrow which brings us almost to breaking point. The crucified Lord chooses them to articulate his own grief and the depth of his pain on behalf of all humanity. This psalm is powerfully expressive of the mystery of his death and resurrection, for its opening words give voice to a most lamentable isolation; midway the prayer gives the atmosphere of actual death and desolation; and then, towards the end, there is a quickening again; the final verses are a dazzling toccata in praise of undying hope and invincible life.

You are the theme of my praise in the Great Assembly ... Those who
seek the Lord will praise him. Long life to their Hearts! ... And my
soul will live for him, my children will serve him; men will proclaim
the Lord to generations still to come, his righteousness to a people yet
unborn. All this he has done (Ps 22: 25-31).

It is in the life of the crucified and Risen Lord that we share and so
our hearts will live. All this he has done out of his high regard and
loving compassion for us. And from his apparently broken heart
and defeated humanity, there escapes the Spirit who fills the
depths of everything; and now death itself is filled with light. The
Spirit, living in our inmost selves, teaches us everything and in-
structs us in the language of hope – the grammar which translates
death from defeat into eternal life.

When we were baptised in Christ Jesus we were baptised in his
death; in other words, when we were baptised we went into
the tomb with him and joined him in death, so that as Christ
was raised from the dead by the Father's glory, we too might
live a new life (Rom 6: 3-4).

The best way to learn a language is to immerse oneself in the cul-
ture and climate where it is in daily use. The same holds true of
our being disciples: students of that 'Wisest Love' expressed in
the logic of Christ crucified and in terms of his death and resurrection. Discipleship is an invitation to live one's life in the shadow of
Calvary; a shadow created in the eternal noon-time splendour of
the Risen Christ. To be baptised is to be immersed in Christ and
over-shadowed by him and thus in constant communion with
him. Discipleship is exposure to the mystery of the Lord's cross
and modelling one's life on it; allowing its message to implant itself in one's life with repercussions of life in abundance.

In the school of Christ we learn that our lives stem from the inex-
haustible energy of love that is the heart of our God; a heart that
is, at the same time, gentle and humble (cf. Mt 11: 29). Although
his life and love are ever creative and renewing the face of the
earth, he is a hidden God who works always on the inside at his
craft of transfiguring and transforming the substance of our
humanity and all reality. That is why the Word was made flesh
and lived among us; so that God could engage us in our plight

from within; so that we would see him, hear him, watch him and touch him and embrace him and so come to know him as one of ourselves (cf. 1 Jn 1: 1-2). In our midst, God-with-us spoke a Word which restored all things, re-consecrating our humanity and reality to its original glorious destiny. Hear it reverberate from the cross, bringing release and newness of purpose to all creation as God Incarnate bows his head and, yielding up his Spirit, utters it: 'It is accomplished.'

CHAPTER FOUR

The mystery of faith:
Ultimate presence

The eucharistic mystery: Communion and Reunion
God pays court to humanity as Emmanuel, God with us. The person who responds to his overtures, by setting out on the journey of faith, will encounter the real and living God in the depths of their being. The glory of God is too overwhelming to be known by the senses which are fragile and defective; that is why God lies hidden in his approaches to humanity. He hides his face for the moment out of compassionate regard for the delicacy of our present condition. Yet his presence is nonetheless real for all that.
When one stands before this real presence, the human person is capable of only one response: a gratitude that spills over into every aspect of our existing. In the presence of such immense love only thanksgiving is appropriate: 'My dear friends, if God loved us so much, we too should love one another' (1 Jn 4:10-11). For a disciple, gratitude to God is no mere duty imposed, but a joyous celebration of who we are. It is an act of love that cannot contain itself, spilling over into all our living. The life of a disciple is thanksgiving and love, expressed in the concrete terms of every word, action and gesture. Believing is stating the mystery of faith in our every action; it is being the means by which God is able to act now, in all the places and situations where I have life and for all the people who engage me there.

To proclaim the mystery of faith is to acknowledge God's presence, to celebrate it and respond to its implications, in a life of faith, hope and love. Therefore, the eucharist is the essence of such a life. The celebration of the eucharist is the summit and source of Christian living, praying and worshipping. The eucharistic mystery is the focal point set by God, bringing us into direct contact, by faith, with the eternal fact of his love for us. The spring-board of all worship and prayer is awareness of the fact that God is really with us. By means of the gift and blessing of the eucharist our hidden God unfolds to us the wonder of who he is. Yes, the eucharist is the festival of the eternal reunion and communion of God and humanity, in Jesus Christ.

What is there so basic to human life as food and drink? They represent much more than the merely material necessities for our physical existence. To share a meal with someone or others, speaks vividly of companionship and intimacy, of the deepening of friendships and the sealing of relationships, of family spirit and communitarian solidarity. All this and infinitely more is what God has in mind in laying the table of the eucharist. At the eucharist, we taste the delights of the table of the Trinity; and so, the divine life we all hold in common is nurtured, deepened and constantly sustained. Gathered around the one table, we hear the saving Word, the loving conversation, by which our knowledge of God is continuously deepened and enriched. Knowledge, not in the sense of assimilating information, but in the manner of lovers who are rapt in one another and who seek to know and speak by means of the heart. Through the eucharist, the true God speaks with us and dines in our company. He addresses us in the manner of a dear friend and shares familial intimacies with us, for we are the people he has chosen as his own possession.

The Eucharist: Sacrament of Life

In the eucharist the entire reality and person of Christ approaches us. He is the way to the Father (Jn 14:7). He has opened a new way for us, a living opening through the curtain, that is to say, his human flesh (Heb 10:20). In other words, we are able to recognise in him one of ourselves – the eldest of many brothers and sisters and thus, our own flesh and blood (Rom 8:29). As such, he is able to take us by the hand into a direct relationship with the living and true God. The curtain, i.e. the veil of estrangement, is rent in shreds by Christ and so the barriers of alienation can be dismantled. 'He has destroyed in his own person the hostility ... through him then, in the one Spirit, we both have free access to the Father (Eph 2:14-18).

The eucharist celebrates the fact that God and humanity are no longer strangers and, indeed, it makes really present God's ultimate gesture of solidarity with us. For it is at Mass that he is, in truth, Emmanuel – God among us! At the eucharist, we are with

Christ who has gone to the very source of our distress. By dying he destroyed our death and by rising he restored our life – he is, therefore, really present at the sorest point of our existence. The eucharist makes effectively present now his eternal victory, his levelling of the wall of death, his demolition of the barricades of sin. With these once seemingly insurmountable obstacles eradicated and the supposedly irreparable damage repaired, he is able to clasp us by the hand in companionship.

The clasp of God's hand enlivens and 'en-Spirits' humanity – the Church is jolted into life and activity, by means of the Lord's cross and resurrection. For it is the same Spirit who raised Christ to life, giving him victory over death, who is poured out upon all believers. It is this same Spirit who animates the community of faith, in its living, praying and worshipping, moving each heart to acknowledge Jesus as Lord (1 Cor 12:3). Particularly at the eucharist, it is the one Spirit, who fills the body, which is the Church, with the breath of divine life; who prays in the assembly of the faithful, combining each heart and being into a harmonious symphony of thanksgiving and praise, to the source of life.

After the resurrection, Jesus appears in the midst of his embryonic Church and he says: 'Peace be with you … after saying this he showed them his hands and his side' (Jn 20:20). He showed them those wounds by which God had once more excavated his way into the midst of the people on whom he had set his heart. From the side of Christ on the cross, there had come flowing blood and water (Jn 19:30-37). This reminds one of Isaiah's prophecy: 'For thus says the Lord, now toward her I send flowing peace like a river and like a stream in spate the glory of the nations … like a son comforted by his mother, so will I comfort you' (Is 66:12). In John's gospel, Christ usually refers to his suffering and death as the hour of glory (cf Jn 12:20-28). This is so because at that hour, when he is lifted up from the earth, God's offer to humanity of life to the full, is made effective and available. Christ is forever glorified in his death because in that act of dying he disarms death forever. He emerges, having engaged the forces of annihilation in mortal combat and from now on there are no doors closed in God's face; there is no area of reality unexposed to that true light and no nook or cranny of the kingdom of darkness, that does not

dissipate before him. The glory of God is the human person fully
alive and our life is to see God! The mystery of faith is the dawning of glory on humanity which awakens us to abundant life. All
who believe have a joy that no-one can ever take from them, because they share the trophy of the risen Christ (Jn 16-22). He has
came back to us! Now it is a reality that, 'anyone who believes in
me, even though that person dies, they will live and whoever
lives and believes in me will never die. Do you believe this? (Jn
11:25-26)

Thus, in the black night of death's shadows, is humanity comforted
by God who rushes to our side as does a mother to her child who
cries out, afraid in the night. Death's sinister shapes are chased
away and a light is kindled which clearly reveals that God's love
for us is stronger than death. The source of that glorious light is
the area around Golgotha, where stands an empty cross and
where lies a garden, in which is found an empty tomb. Amidst
this scene, there stands a New Man from whose glorified humanity
there comes flowing upon creation, a mighty torrent which rein-
vigorates, revives, refreshes and resuscitates. It is the living water
of the Spirit, able to erupt at last, in the history of a broken human
race. For Christ has unsealed it and by his wounds, the precious
gifts of the Spirit can now irrigate our humanity and the world,
causing us to be a New Creation and empowering us to be, once
more, children of God, in name and in fact!

The Lord's cross and resurrection has clearly manifested how
much God values us. The extent to which he loves us is the deriva-
tive source of our dignity. Christ has made us free indeed! He re-
makes humanity at it is meant to be; since it is from him that we
receive the spirit of new birth and adoption. In Christ, we are co-
opted into the community of the Trinity and so, we are no longer
slaves of anyone or anything, but daughters and sons, and if children, then heirs, by God's own act! (Gal 4:7)

What marvels the Lord has worked for us, indeed we are glad!
Therefore, my soul proclaims the greatness of the Lord and my
spirit exults in God my saviour ... for the Almighty has done
great things for me. It is right to give him thanks and praise for
these wondrous realities and such overwhelming blessings. He
has no need of our praise yet because he loves us and delights to

be with us, he enjoys sitting down with us at the eucharistic table where, together with him, we contemplate and relive the sacrifice of Christ, who loved us and gave himself up for us.

The eucharist is the source and summit of our Christian lives. Yet what is God saying and doing for us at the eucharist? Let us look a little more into the depths of the word itself: eucharist. It stems from the Greek, *eucharistia*, which means to give thanks. It was the word chosen by the early Christians to translate the Hebrew word, *berakoth*, blessing. For the Jews, the basic form of all prayer was blessing. In the Latin, to bless, translates as *benedicere*, to speak well of – and so to bless the Lord is to speak well of him; to speak of him with love, praise and thanksgiving, for all the gifts and goodness which are signs of his saving, loving presence. Such sentiments are powerfully expressed in the book of Psalms, which are peppered with invitations such as:

> Bless the Lord my soul, from the depths of my being bless his holy name; bless the Lord my soul, never forget all his acts of kindness (Ps 103:1-2).

> Give thanks to the Lord for he is good, for his faithful love endures forever (Ps 118:1).

Therefore, it is possible to state, briefly and simply, that the eucharist is the great thanksgiving prayer of God's people. It is prayed along with Christ: through him, with him, in the unity brought about in the One Spirit, for all the blessings of life and salvation that come to us from the creator Father. Those blessings are we grateful for, which find their ultimate expression in the unspeakable gift of his Son, so much did he love the world. 'For in him (Christ) is found the yes to all God's promises and, therefore, it is through him that we answer 'Amen' to give praise to God' (2 Cor 1:20).

Do this in memory of me
At the Last Supper, as Jesus kept the passover with his disciples, he faced the inevitability of his imminent betrayal, rejection, crucifixion and death. It was a death he freely accepted out of love for humanity, so that he might draw all peoples, generations and times to himself (Jn 12:32). In spite of the anguish and distress we see him afflicted with in the garden of Olives, he is able to set his

face like flint, as his hour draws near (Is 50:4-7). Christ approaches the cross with faith-filled confidence in the Father who, as Psalm 16:9-11 promises *'will not leave his soul among the dead, nor allow his holy one to experience corruption.'*

In his passion and death, the Lord meets head on, on its own ground and in full battle, the ancient darkness and the power of death. By dying, he goes into the very heart of that 'ravine as dark as death' (Ps 23:4), and confronts all the terrors in 'that land of a shadow as dark as death' (Is 9:1). In the place of fear, he has blazed forth as the eternal Light, 'a light the darkness cannot overcome' (Jn 1:5). At the eucharist, the splendour of that invisible light is shed upon our faith and our existence is filled with the real presence of him who by dying has destroyed death and who by rising has restored life: he whose glorious return we await with songs of joyful hope!

On the threshold of those days, the words and actions of Jesus at the Last Supper, would be of central importance and immense consequence for the Church, ever after. What we witness in the Upper Room is a mighty work of Jesus the prophet; we experience there a wondrous gesture of the eternal God, in whose heart is present always, every person who ever was, is and shall be; he who is today as he was yesterday and as he will be forever. Christ, the first and the last, the beginning and the end, is able to anticipate and make effectively present among his disciples, at the final passover of the old order, his supreme action of love; the saving, life-giving event of his cross and resurrection. He communes with them and draws them together in a bond of love that is expressed in word and gesture as he leaves an example for them to copy (Jn 13:1-16).

His last wish is that they love one another in the same way and to the same extent as he had loved them (Jn 15:12-13). In order to empower them to love as he loves, he makes present the gift of gifts – his very self. His words come back to mind as recorded by John:

> Whoever eats my flesh and drinks my blood lives in me and I live in that person. As the living Father sent me and I draw life from the Father, so whatever eats me will also draw life from me (Jn 6:55-56).

In the Upper Room among his friends, Jesus brings into existence the means by which we will draw life from him, until he comes again.

God, in Christ, has be-friended us and become our companion. Through the mystery of the eucharist, we are enveloped in Trinitarian love. This means that the Father, Son and Spirit have made room for us in their company, setting an extra space for us at their table. In doing so, they make us sharers in their dynamic and life-giving relationship. At the eucharistic celebration we are more than just honoured guests: the flavour of the encounter is familial and convivial. Therefore, our standing at the Lord's table is as daughters and sons, with all the rights and privileges of a first born and thus, heirs! The prophetic action of Jesus at the Last Supper, encapsulates the great event of salvation which he is on the threshold of consummating. His words and deeds in that Upper Room were prophetic in the truly biblical sense. They brought into the reality of the present moment, the happenings to take place at Golgotha on the following day. He made present, in anticipatory joy, the dawning of the first day of the week truly a day of all days! For not even time itself could contain moments such as were soon to transpire.

The main texts of scripture which relate to the institution of the eucharist are found in Luke 22:19-20, 1 Cor 11:23-24, Mt 26:26-28 and Mk 14:22-24. The cornerstone of our understanding of the eucharist are the words of Christ recorded in the Lucan and Pauline accounts – 'Do this as a memorial of me.' The word 'memorial' is of profound relevance, for it is a deeply significant word in the context of the passover liturgy at the time of Our Lord. It was this passover festival that Jesus and his disciples were keeping as they reclined at table, on the eve of his passion.

The passover feast was the celebration of the exodus from Egypt (Ex 12:1-14). The exodus was the sign and event, *par excellence*, which established God's saving presence for the people he had especially chosen and called. The exodus event was God's hearing of their cry of distress and his championing of their cause against the oppressive evil of their situation in Egypt (Ex 3:78-10). The deliverance from Egypt was the outstanding sacrament of God's nearness, which had branded itself indelibly onto the communal consciousness of the Jewish people. Remembrance of the exodus was crucial, because their entire identity as a nation was invested in that event. To forget the exodus would be to forget who they are and thus, become obliterated; swallowed up by the nations that surrounded them, with their immoral practices and false gods.

Indeed to forget the Lord and become like pagans would always be a real danger for Israel, a temptation they would find difficult to resist. Their frequent and protracted falls into infidelity and waywardness, were inevitably the occasion of national catastrophe and the exile which dispersed them to the four winds: they had turned aside from God's law and this was a highly significant factor in their ruination. The commandments were the means by which the special relationship between God and Israel, along with its communal implications, were protected and sustained. Enshrined in this covenant agreement was the principle of life as God – given and, as such, calling for a response of the entire person, heart, soul, mind and strength – in love for the creator. The law was also, in a sense, a divine bill of rights which safeguarded the value and dignity of each individual; it was also a communal code of conduct designed for the protection of the defenceless and the poor; as well as for the right ordering of inter-personal and inter-group relationships. It was, of course, a solemn agreement between God and his people.

Forgetfulness, complacency and a tendency to exploit the very members of society they were commanded to guard, were the root causes of Israel's constant failure to honour God's law and keep their side of the agreement. It was this scenario that gave the missions of the prophets a sense of urgency. Remembering and sometimes being shocked into remembrance was, therefore, integral to this relationship between God and Israel. The yearly festival of the passover was the remembrance of the exodus. However, here we reach a difficulty of translation, a language barrier that will only be overcome, if we keep in mind that our use of the term 'remembrance' and our concept of 'memorial' is insipid in comparison and a pale shadow of what the Hebrews understood by remembering.

The passover, you see, was no mere looking back to the exodus as a historical event, inevitably shrouded in the mists of time. It was its 'living memorial'! A memorial alive, imbued and on fire with the reality of what actually occurred in the past event. For a Jewish person, even today, to remember in the context of the passover, is, in a very real sense, to relive the experience being recalled in word and ritual. It is believed that the power and reality of the past event is inextricably woven into the fabric of the present moment, by the actions in which it is called to mind. Therefore, at the passover, God continues to lead his people from slavery and oppression, to freedom and new life; he does this for them in a way that is real, powerful and dynamic, as they give him thanks in the successive generations.

We who live in the day of the new and everlasting covenant, know that all these wondrous signs and events experienced by our ancestors in faith, were but a foreshadowing of and a prelude to that day of days – the Lord's day which we are glad to see! For now, God has finally and ultimately made known the full significance of who he is; for now he has become, in the history and experience of the human race, Emmanuel – the Word made flesh living among us! We can now see his eternal glory reflected in the human face of Christ: 'For now, in our own time, the final days, God has spoken to us in the person of his Son, through whom he made the ages' (Heb 1:1-2).

CHAPTER FIVE

God among us:
A real and abiding presence

The Mass: New passover, living memorial
At the Last Supper, as his earthly ministry drew to a close, as the days of his life-giving death and glorious resurrection were approaching, Jesus took bread: he blessed it, broke it and gave it to his disciples saying, 'Take it, eat, this is my Body. He then passed to them the cup of blessing and said, 'This is my Blood ...' (Mk 14:22-25): 'Do this as a memorial of me' (Lk 22:19).

It is, therefore, at the Lord's instructions, that the eucharist is celebrated, offered and received. It is the Lord's living memorial, in which is vividly recalled and brought to bear on the present moment, his death endured for our salvation, his glorious resurrection and ascension into heaven. The eucharist is no less than the Lord's offering of himself, once and for all on the cross, made really present in our today. As such, it is a holy and living sacrifice, for it is the prayer of Christ the High Priest: he who was dead but who, behold, is now alive for evermore (Rev 1:17-19). The Mass is the plea of Christ our brother, who is forever at the Father's right hand, our intercessor (Rom 8:33-35).

We believe, as Catholics, that the Mass is the new passover. We have seen how, for the people of Israel, the old passover was the living memorial of what God did in delivering them from injustice and crushing oppression. The passover celebration ratified, renewed and represented in every generation, that momentous exodus occasion of his saving, faithful love. At the Last Supper however, Jesus altered the entire significance of the passover memorial, by bringing it to its logical conclusion and fulfilment: from now on, it would be in memory of him! The event which the deliverance from Egypt prefigured, was about to be effected through his cross and resurrection by which Jesus liberates us from the slavery of sin and the ultimate tyranny of death. In one place in scripture, his passion and death are referred to as, 'his passing which he was to accomplish in Jerusalem' (Lk 9:31): the Greek text translates the word 'passing' as *exodus*.

Jesus is our brother. This means that, with him, we are in direct relationship with the Father. Because he is our elder brother, he does not leave our side but goes before us, as like a new Moses, leading the way. He is the great pioneer of our salvation, who blazes the trail through the wilderness of sin, the desert of alienation from God (Heb 10:19, 12:1-2). He removes all obstacles and barriers in our path, for he is the way. He inaugurates the way in our flesh to eternal life and glory, enabling us to passover with him into the family circle of the Holy Trinity: all of us thus, daughters and sons of one Father and, therefore, sisters and brothers of one another in Christ, and held together in relationship by one Spirit.

At Mass, we relive, we celebrate, we give thanks, for all that God has done for us in his Son. We proclaim the Lord's death until he comes (1 Cor 11:23-25); for in his dying and rising, Christ has overwhelmed all the anti-human forces which militate against and seek to destroy humanity. For this we give thanks through Christ, with him and in him. With Christ as our companion, we approach the doorway of the eternal where God awaits us. In Christ, who is our God made visible, we can draw close to the living God and offer him our worship in spirit and in truth. True Christian worship is the response of those who have within their hearts the Spirit whom the Father sends in Christ's name to teach us everything and remind us of all he said to us (Jn 14:26). Christian worship is the response of a human being to God's truth revealed in Christ; it is the acknowledgement of his sovereignty manifested in adoration, thanksgiving, petition and, consequently, concrete action in practical service to our sisters and brothers. To worship in spirit and in truth, is our 'yes', our great 'Amen', to the reality of God among us and the revelation of his truth, his love and the plans of his heart for each of us. The Spirit of love, who dwells in our hearts, unfolds to us the wonderful truth of who God is and who we are: the eucharistic celebration is our joining with Christ in one, great 'Thank you' to the Father. At Mass we are with Christ, worshipping in his company; we gather around the risen Lord, who is among us in a real, unique and wondrous manner.

'It is the Lord.' Such was the acclamation of faith made by the apostles and other disciples, when he appeared to them in visible form, after the resurrection. The entire purpose of the Lord's cross and the resurrection is that all of life becomes a passover experience, an exodus journey from the visible to the invisible, a faith pilgrimage towards the God we are, as yet, unable to see. Be that as it may however, the hidden reality of his near presence, brightens our way and sustains our steps. What God accomplished for our ancestors – those pioneering pilgrims of Moses and Aaron's day – by walking at their head, a pillar of cloud by day and a column of fire by night; and feeding them with the manna he rained down so generously for them, he does for us now, in an even more wonderful manner. By means of the blessing of the eucharist, God actually abides with us as companion and accompanies us as fellow-pilgrim.

It is the Lord! Luke recounts how, after the resurrection, their eyes were opened and they recognised him at the breaking of the bread (Lk 24:35). In the strength of that bread, they recovered their enthusiasm and developed a joyous energy they thought had perished along with their hopes, only a short while previously. After all, had he not promised? 'I will not leave you orphans; I will come back to you. In a short while the world will no longer see me; but you will see me, because I live and you will live (Jn 14:18-19). The life of a Christian is inextricably linked with Christ; it is living in the manner of a continuous passing over into the sphere of the invisible realities of faith, where we meet Christ and draw life from him. This mode of seeing, however, transcends the sensual and the visible and is all the more profoundly real than it ever could be at that level.

In the paschal mystery of his death and resurrection, Christ has now passed over into the eternal realm and, therefore, is no longer to be found only in one place, at a certain time and at a given period in history. Christ has eradicated the demarcation lines that existed between time and eternity and so the joy of his risen life knows no bounds and no limits. He is now able to embrace the entire community of faith in every nook and cranny of the earth and satisfy their hunger with the Bread of Life to the full – his living flesh. It was at the moment that the risen Christ took bread, said the blessing and then broke and handed it to them, that the early disciples' eyes were opened and they recognised him (Lk 24:30-31). If we too, his contemporary disciples, were to prize open the eyes of our faith, then the celebration of the eucharist would never be a boring ritual: we would see it as it really is – the Easter feast of joy and life without limit, presided over by the risen Christ, whose name is Emmanuel. It is from him that we draw life and thus the eucharist is central and pivotal to our being disciples.

'It is the Lord': The faith of the Church in the real presence
of the Risen Lord in the eucharist
The unshakeable faith of the Church, from its very beginnings, in the Lord's real eucharistic presence, is on the strength of his own teaching in the gospel and on the practice of the apostolic faith communities (*cf* Mt 26:26-29; Mk 14:22-25; Lk 22:19-20; Jn 6:51-58; 1 Cor 10:15-17; 1 Cor 1:23-27). As we celebrate his living memorial, he comes among us by the action of the Holy Spirit, in all his power as saviour, Lord and redeemer. The reality of his cross and resurrection breaks in upon our time, space and place.

Sometimes other Christians express uncertainty about what Catholics mean when they speak of the *sacrifice* of the Mass. The eucharistic sacrifice, it must be clearly understood, is not, in any sense, a repetition of Calvary at any level. The Lord does not suffer and die all over again, each time the Mass is celebrated. For truly, we also believe, that it is finished (Jn 19:30), and that Christ has offered one single sacrifice for sins and then taken his place forever at the right hand of God (Heb 10:11-12, 14).

The Mass, however, proclaims the Lord's death until he comes (1 Cor 11:26). It is one and the same sacrifice as was offered on the cross, made really present now and in every generation until the Lord comes. It would be inconceivable that the fact and reality of the Lord's saving victory over sin and death could become relegated to the purely historical realm. It is certainly the faith of most Christian believers, of all traditions, that God intended them to be effective, relevant, and above all, present for all time and all people. All Christians firmly believe that the blessings of salvation achieved for us by Christ, are ever available for us, as in an eternal moment. This exactly expresses our faith and understanding of the sacrifice of the Mass. The Mass does not, indeed cannot, repeat Calvary; neither does it add to or subtract from it. It makes the Lord's saving work really present now and unites us with the fact of his love, expressed in the event of his death and resurrection. The Mass perpetuates the reality of the sacrifice of Christ, by means of which we passover into the Father's love forever.

'I am with you always until the end of time' (Mt 28:20). Therefore, the eucharist is a promise kept, but in what a surprising and outstanding manner. In regard to Christ's real presence in the eucharist, we say unequivocally and quite explicity, in faith, 'it is the Lord' (Jn 21:7). For just over a millennium, such was the simple and unquestioned faith of the Church. As time moved on however this incomprehensible mystery of faith was more and more called into question. Misconceptions began to multiply.

From approximately the eleventh century onwards, two extreme positions began to develop. On the one hand, there was the reduction of the real presence in the eucharist to a crude, almost cannibalistic, physicalism; and to the other extreme, a perception of Christ's presence as purely symbolic, so much so, that the reality of his presence was effectively watered down or denied altogether. In response to this dual manifestation of a basic misunderstanding of Christ's eucharistic presence, theologians and teachers of the faith had to reflect ever more deeply on this wonder of wonders, in order to enrich the people of God in their appreciation of it.

The Lord's eucharistic presence is ultimately, of course, inexplicable and incomprehensible. We believe it firmly on the strength of his word and testimony alone. Over the course of centuries, however, the ancient faith of the Christian community was re-articulated and reiterated in ways that are perennially valid and useful. As a result of much reflection and deliberation, the true teaching on the eucharist was re-expressed, as a middle way between the extremes of crude physicalism and pure symbolism.

The Lord, in the eucharist, is really present *under the appearance* of bread and wine. In so far as the senses are concerned, there occurs no change whatsoever in the elements of bread and wine. However, what is brought about by the Lord's word and the power of his Holy Spirit, is an entire change, in a way that is beyond the senses to grasp. For there is effected a change of the whole substance of bread into the substance of the body of Christ and of the whole substance of wine into his blood: this change has been thus termed *transubstantiation* – the changing of one substance into another. Such a work of invisible refashioning, could only be wrought by God, the architect of all realities and the author of all that exists.

Transubstantiation means the changing of one substance into another. It is the term employed by the Church in an attempt to describe the marvellous occurrence, whereby bread and wine are really changed into the entire person of Christ, substantially present. The word *substance*, however, can give the wrong impression in this context. We are inclined to think of *substance* as a purely material entity; for example, we speak of having had a *substantial* meal, or winning a *substantial* sum of money. When we speak of the real and *substantial* presence of Christ in the Most Blessed Sacrament, however, we are referring to *substance* without accidents or visible manifestation. The word *substance* derives from the Latin *sub stans* which means to stand under. In the eucharist, therefore, we worship the Lord and share in his Divine Life, who is present *standing under the appearance of* bread and wine.

We now know, as a proven fact of atomic physics, that there is much more to material form than meets the eye and that the world is formed ultimately from webs or fields of indivisible points of energy which defy qualitative or quantative analysis – in other words, *substance* without *accidents*. To enable us, therefore, in some way, to fumble towards an apprehension of the mystery of the real presence, it might help to understand substance as the soul of matter, as what lies under its exterior, accidental and visible manifestation. Take also, for example, the case of the human body itself. It is a marvellous complexity of cellular structures and chemical interactions; but unless it is animated by that mysterious energy of life, the soul, it becomes merely a decaying mass of substances returning to atomic matter. The soul is that invisible dimension of the human person that cannot be weighed, described or dissected. The soul is that reality of the person which is as real as the physique, but which cannot be known empirically; just as substance is that portion of matter which stands under its obvious attributes.

The Catholic doctrine of transubstantiation is a profound genu-
flection, in silent wonder and adoring awe, before the reality of
him who stands at the heart of all that is; who has designed and
constructed all things visible and invisible; who, in the mystery of
his Love, seeks to bind himself to us inseparably, as the very substance of who and what we are. At the eucharist, therefore, there
occurs a real change, but not one that can be apprehended by the
senses. On the surface of the bread and wine, in so far as sight,
taste, smell and touch are concerned, nothing gives the appearance of having been disturbed or rearranged. In the depths, however, the unseen God has effected a new work; an entire re-
ordering; a veritable re-creation.

Bread and wine are representative of food and drink which provide human beings with strength of limb, health of mind, cheer-
fulness of heart and vitality of body. At the eucharist, these token
gifts are transformed and thereby become the vehicle of that energy of Divine Life; the living presence of him who raises our spirits
to Eternal Life. At the eucharist, it is Christ himself who speaks
and at once, according to his Word made fruitful by the sanctify-
ing action of the Creator Spirit, mere bread and wine, those mundane and humble commodities, are endowed with unfathomable
depths of infinity, so that the Eternal One can hide in them; so that
he can fashion new links with us and foster a new unity among
us, by our sharing with him in the one Bread and Cup; so that he
can have access to the inner sanctum of the human spirit; so that
he can be really present there as the One who transfigures, *tran-
substantiates*, our frail humanity; so that he can make us strong for
the carrying of a weight of eternal glory and give us already a
foretaste of the heavenly Banquet, where we will be filled with the
utter fullness of God; and inebriated with the best Wine of resurrection joy, being stored and fermented for us in our true home, in
the depths of the Trinity.

It is always difficult for creatures of flesh and blood to try and
conceive of realities invisible and imperceptible to our sense nature. Difficult? Yes. Impossible? No. We are now in that place
where God hides and waits for us: the realm of faith. The senses,
with which we perceive, discover and assess the material world,
are useless to us here. In this domain, one must put out one's

hand, in order to be led by a way in which we know nothing. The light of faith will burn only in an atmosphere of trust and abandonment, only then will the radiance of God's nearness become obvious to our hearts.

Transubstantiation is a difficult word. It treats of sights unseen; it reveals a God who is the substance of all that is; who is able to dwell in that which is mundane and in the midst of ordinariness. This is a God who comes too close for comfort. But his name is Emmanuel! He is come to transfigure, in its entirety, the substance of weak nature, by the infusion of his superabundant life. In order to contemplate the marvel of the eucharist, one must take a step in faith beyond what lies on the surface – mere bread and wine. For in the depths of this mystery there is, really and truly present, the entire person of Jesus Christ, truly God and truly man, crucified, risen and glorified. Thus:

> 'There remains no room for doubting that all the faithful of Christ, in accordance with the perpetual custom of the Catholic Church, must venerate this most holy sacrament with the worship which is due to the true God. Nor is it less to be adored because it was instituted by Christ the Lord to be received (Mt 26:26). For in it we believe that the same God is present whom the eternal Father brought into the world saying: 'Let all the angels of God worship him (Heb 1:6. Ps 97:7), whom the Magi fell down to worship (Mt 2:11), and finally, whom the apostles adored in Galilee as scripture testifies (Mt 28:17)' (*Decree on the Most Holy Eucharist*, 13th Session of Trent, chap. V).

But some may ask, is not this intolerable language? How could anyone accept it? Is it not at total variance with reason? (*cf* Jn 6:52-66)

Only faith can guarantee ... the existence of the realities that at present remain unseen (Heb 11:1).

The Church accepts Christ's words and responds to them in faith. Illumined by faith, we gain a radically new perspective on reality. When the infinite mystery of the love of God had begun to dawn on the human race, God introduced himself to Moses as follows:

> 'in a flame burning from the middle of a bush. Moses looked; there was the bush blazing, but the bush was not being burnt up.' He revealed his name to Moses: 'I am he who is'.

From the heart of that burning bush, God begins to unveil the glory of who he is and the significance that this will hold for us. He is, in fact, the only and ultimate reality who has set the raw material of creation, of life and of living, aflame with his presence (cf Ex 3:1-6).

He is present already at the heart of all created reality and being: for it is his loving us which bestows in the first case and then sustains, the gift of existence. Yet although our God is a consuming fire of passionate, loving intensity, he is, at the same time, infinitely tender courtesy. The bush, although it shows forth his presence, is not consumed or devoured, by the eternal glorious splendour it makes present. And neither are we!

Although he has lavished his love on us, in letting us be called his children (1 Jn 3:1-2), he respects us so much that he woos and allures, invites and calls. He created us, not to smother or overwhelm our being with his infinity, but to share his joy with us and make us heirs to his eternal glory (Rom 8:17). Already, even in the delicacy of our present fragility, we are empowered to be '... like mirrors reflecting the glory of Lord ... being transformed into the image we reflect, in brighter and brighter glory ...' (2 Cor 3:17-18) 'It is God who said 'let light shine out of darkness', that has shone into our hearts to enlighten them with the knowledge of God's glory, the glory on the face of Christ' (2 Cor 4:6).

The relationship God invites us to enter into with him is characterised by faith. Faith involves a looking beyond appearances and a trusting beyond experiences. It challenges us to look at the world with new eyes; it dares us to allow ourselves to meet God there; to recognise as did the poet, that: 'the world is charged with the grandeur of God. It will flame out, like shining from shook foil.'

The eucharistic presence of the risen Christ flames out from the mundane humility of bread and wine, changed at the word of him who spoke in the beginning, 'Let there be light.' Love changes the ordinariness of what represents food and drink, by calling it something entirely different: 'This is my body. This is my blood.' The real presence of our Lord in the eucharist invites us to take a step beyond what is obvious and perceptible only to the senses. Christ calls us into the light of faith where we are enabled to see and to kneel before the hidden reality of truth proclaiming along with those earlier disciples: 'It is the Lord.' Yes it is true, the Lord is indeed risen and is among us. We have recognised him in the breaking of bread.

After they had recognised him, the gospel relates that he vánished from their sight. That is why those who follow him must have eyes for the invisible, in order to meet Christ and draw life from the bread that is ever new; the bread which makes our hidden selves strong with the substance of our unseen God. As we contemplate the Lord living among us in the eucharist, let us hear in this context, the teaching of St Paul: 'And so, we have no eyes for things that are visible, but only for the things that are invisible; for the visible things last only for a while and the invisible things are eternal' (2 Cor 4:18).

CHAPTER 6

Communion and action:
Becoming what we receive

The eucharist: 'God living among his people
The eucharist is God's reply to our human need for him by which
he addresses our poverty and nothingness without him. At the
eucharist we are honoured guests of the Trinity at a banquet of
'rich food and fine wines' (Is 25:6). Such delectable fare is not, of
course, apparent to any of the senses. For we have seen that the
eucharist contains our hidden God who alone can satisfy the hungry heart and quench the thirst of our yearning spirits.

From the eucharistic vantage point, we see the past, the present
and the future, in the perspective of God's ever-presence. For it is
there that we are seated at table with our God: we hang on to his
every word, which awakens and sustains life within us. He
imparts to us his wisdom, which sheds light on our pilgrim path,
saving us from many pitfalls and potholes. The eucharist is a veritable *tour de force* of the presence of God which engages us at every
level of our being. Not only does Christ offer us the very gift of
himself, in the life-giving bread and the saving cup, but in our
very gathering together, we are already face to face with him in
one another. At the eucharist, the Body of Christ – each one of us –
comes in from its labours for the sake of the kingdom, for our
meeting with Christ our strength.

At Mass, the priest and people together celebrate God's presence
made tangible in Christ, by the power of the Spirit who fills the
universe. Having acclaimed the word of God, having listened to it
with faith and welcomed it with a receptive and generous heart,
those hearts should then be ready to welcome into their depths,
the Word who continues to be made flesh in our flesh, through
the eucharistic gift of himself to us. The eucharist is truly a feast of
God's generosity, in which he gives us his own life super-
abundantly, that we might be fit, healthy of spirit and ready for
action.

For Catholics, the celebration of the eucharist is of central significance and profound consequence to the Christian life. It is the
fount and summit of our discipleship. At the eucharist, we are
drawn by the Lord into the great mystery of his death and resurrection – what we call the paschal mystery. We become partakers
in that mystery and are given power to live it out each day.

The term 'Paschal Mystery' describes the entire reality of Christian
worship, prayer and living. Yet, for many, it remains a mysterious
concept. How can it be put simply?

The paschal mystery means that God is now one of us. He has
found us, caught up with us at last and embraced us. Never again
will he let us go! The paschal mystery is the reality that God is our
companion, in Christ, who provides us with the eucharistic food
of eternal life, as we walk en route to the kingdom, with the wind
of the Spirit ever at our backs. The paschal mystery means that,
with the risen Christ, we are able to step over all obstacles and
barriers, that keep us away from the fullness of life. Christ's cross
has demolished the wall of sin and death; and we, through baptism, are immersed in an unstoppable torrent of resurrected life
which revives our human dignity, opening our eyes, once more,
to the wondrous truth of who we are. The paschal mystery has
swept death away forever and the joy of irrepressible life is renewing all creation. Our mission, as his partners and apprentices,
is to be such springs of living water, as will flood the world and
our communities with his presence. We, after all, are his agents,
the living cells of his body.

At the eucharist, Christ is among us as one serves, offering his life
as a ransom for many (Lk 22:7; Mk 20:28). It makes present for us,
now, Christ's sacrifice of his entire self for me. And so, each time
we eat the Bread of Life and drink the Blessing Cup, we associate
ourselves intimately with that offering of the Lord. We are saying
'Amen, yes, so be it', to his invitation to a life of committed and
self-sacrificing love and service. For Christ has left us as example
that we are to copy: an example expressed in the simple gesture of
washing feet and a call to do the same for one another (Jn 13:1-15).

Strengthened by the gift of the eucharist, we can say 'Amen' to
this challenge to die to self-love. We say 'Amen' to the reality that

we too must allow ourselves to be broken, poured out and offered in service to all our sisters and brothers. The Christian life, after all, is a sharing in the life of Christ from the moment we are plunged into him in baptism. We were carried to the Church in the arms of our parents and, likely as not, borne away from the font howling for all we were worth; baffled at this sudden intrusion, this rude awakening, this splash of cold water. Yes, there is something in the experience of baptism that has all the connotations of a short, sharp shock. The word itself – baptism – derives from the Greek term for immersion or taking the plunge.

But that is how God always likes to work. He likes to seize upon people, take them by surprise, pluck them out of obscurity and thrust them into the light. Is that not how a young boy, David, minding his sheep and his own business, suddenly found himself grabbed and anointed king? And what of the unfortunate Jeremiah? 'Ah Lord, I do not know how to speak. I am only a youth!' And then one day, as Jesus walked along, he came across a man who had been blind since birth: without so much as a 'by your leave' and without asking his permission, Jesus gave him the light of his eyes (Jn 9:1-41). Sometimes, you see, love has to make the first move and that is what God has done with us; when we were baptised, he took the initiative in love: 'For we were darkness once, but now we are light in the Lord; be like children of light, for the effects of the light are seen in complete goodness and right living and truth' (Eph 5:8).

The Mass and our lives
Sharing the life of Christ inevitably entails sharing his suffering, so as to share his glory (Rom 8:17). Thus at the eucharist we offer our entire selves with Christ and we pray that our sacrifice will be acceptable to the Father. Through him, with him, in him: we unite ourselves to Christ so that, more and more, we might be transformed into his likeness.

At Mass, we offer to God bread and wine, which earth has given and human hands have made. We thus offer him the raw materials of our existence which speak of the fruits of the earth, the sweat of our brow, our disappointments and successes, our achievements and failures, our tears and our laughter, our sorrows and our joys. We ask God to send the Holy Spirit upon the gifts of bread and wine and make them holy, so that they may become for us, the body and blood of his Son. Just as we believe that the bread and wine is transformed into the risen Christ, with only the appearances remaining, so we pray that in receiving these wondrous presents of God's love, we might also be changed in our substance and become more and more like him. Thus we will be able to allow him to be really present in the world, on the streets of our towns, our neighbourhoods and in our homes, through the medium of our human lives of Christian witness and love.

It is by your love for one another that everyone will recognise you as my disciples (Jn 13:35).

Christ asks us to love one another as he loves us. The Spirit, who has been poured out on us so generously, at our baptism and confirmation, makes it possible for us not only to live with God's own life, but to love with his own love. Before he left our visible sight, Christ made it clear that 'the world can never accept this Spirit of truth because it neither sees him nor knows him.' But, he tells the disciples, you know him 'because he is with you, he is in you' (Jn 14:16-17). When Jesus was glorified in his death and resurrection, it soon became necessary for him to leave us in the material sense. He did this to our advantage so that his presence would no longer be confined within the limits of Palestine at that period in history. When his hour of glory dawns, he transcends his earthly body, so that his all-pervading presence might fill all that is; that God may be all in all (1 Cor 15:28).

His glory is now concealed from our sense eyes. We are now incapable, as we stand, of looking into his face. Yet still he assures us: I am with you always until the end of the ages. Therefore, we are asked to train the interior eye of faith, which alone can perceive the invisible realities of truth, so that we will be fit and ready to see him when at last he appears. The Spirit who lives in our hearts, gradually works on the eyes of the heart and enables them to become accustomed to seeing through a glass darkly (1 Cor 13:12). Through the in-dwelling of the Spirit, we are able to continue knowing Christ with the interior vision of faith. As receivers of the Spirit, we can therefore transmit Christ and present him in the world by our actions.

It is in this way that the Father's will continues to be done by the Son, working through all those who are attuned to him; all those who are, even now, here on earth, in communion with the Trinity, by virtue of their being daughters and sons of the Father, along with Christ, the eldest of many brothers and sisters (Rom 8:30). We are united with him who is first-born from the dead (Rev 1:5) and have received from him the spirit of adoption that makes us, in name and in fact, God's own children and joint heirs with Christ, provided that we share his suffering so as to share his glory (Rom 8:14-17).

For the Church, the eucharist is the very source of our strength and the means by which we are enabled to *be* the Church. The eucharist brings us into direct contact, face to face, heart to heart, by faith, with Christ who is the head of the body, the Church, and we are his living parts (Col 1:18). The eucharist bonds us together in unity and love and is the well-spring of the Church's vitality. By it, we are energised for our mission in the world, of continuing the work of God in Christ – a saving work, a healing work, a task of recreating, restoring and transforming, by the power of Christ and in his Spirit of love.

The post-communion prayer from the Liturgy for the feast of St Augustine (August 28th) prays:

> Lord, make us holy by our sharing at the table of Christ. As members of his body, help us to become what we have received.

Help us to become what we have received. Literally, may we become holy communion to one another and all we meet. In other words, may our lives be a point of contact, a place of encounter with Christ, where his presence and his influence is felt in our practical action for justice; in the helping hand and the shoulder to lean on; in the gesture of forgiveness and the dismantling of barriers, which are the cause of distrust, fear and pain to the human family, both at global and local levels.

The eucharist requires that we make of our lives a living offering of praise and thanks, united with Christ; a life which holds nothing back. A life which proclaims the Lord's cross and resurrection; a life which cries the gospel of death destroyed and life restored. At the eucharist, we celebrate the Lord's deliverance of us from fear, self-love, sin and death itself; and in so doing, we relive our salvation. We share the food of life eternal, the bread which contains the substance of eternity and which nourishes our development towards that full stature and potential which will be ours in resurrection. We are a eucharistic people and, in the company of Christ, we are continuously passing over from death to the fullness of life.

At the end of Mass, we are exhorted, 'Go in peace to love and serve the Lord!' We are thus obliged to allow the eucharist access to all areas of our existence – it must overflow into my daily living. The privilege of having the holy eucharist reserved in our churches for contemplative adoration, allows us to gaze constantly into the depths of the love of God; to look into the eyes of Emmanuel. The reality of our eucharistic Lord's presence with us however, is not only a mystery to be adored, but a drama to be enacted each day: a drama which unfolds in the daily scenes of our lives and in which we are the main players. Not that we are merely acting a part or playing a role, for we are radically engaged in keeping the reality of Christ to the forefront of every thought, word and action. Our lives are substantially changed into a living memorial of him, as we strive to live always, through him, with him, and in him; manifesting in our life together as the community of faith, the unity of the Spirit, so that the world may taste and see the fruits of love and, therefore, come to believe in the Father. The eucharist is a celebration of our tangible companionship with Christ who walks with us, by word and sacrament, towards the kingdom. As we journey with him, we recount, in grateful thanks, his loving mercy and constant fidelity in the past; we sing joyful songs of his nearness to us now; and this enables us to look to the horizon of the future with trustful courage and confident hope. An image comes to mind of how, in the early Church, newly baptised members of the Church would sing the twenty-third psalm, as they left the baptismal waters to approach the eucharist for the first time. They sang it with the water still dripping off them, with the sacred Chrism still glistening wetly upon their heads:

The Lord is my shepherd, I lack nothing.
In meadows of green grass he lets me lie.
To the waters of repose he leads me,
There he revives my soul.
He guides me by paths of virtue
for the sake of his name.

Though I pass through a gloomy valley,
I fear no harm:
beside me your rod and your staff are there,
to hearten me.

You prepare a table before me
under the eyes of my enemies:
you anoint my head with oil,
my cup brims over.

Ah, how goodness and kindness pursue me,
every day of my life;
my home, the house of the Lord, as long as I live!'

In the strength of this food, we will at last reach the house of the Lord, where the Father will dance and exult over us, on what will become a day of unending festival and a banquet of life to the full!

We are eucharistic people

There is a very special happiness when family and friends enjoy a meal together. There is a pleasure not only in the food that nourishes the body, but particularly in the conversation and time spent together. Even after the dishes have been cleared away, it is not uncommon to find nurturing and feeding of a much higher level begin, as the guests relax, listen, converse and generally enjoy one another's company. The eucharist is such a meal. It is the table dressed and prepared by the Father's hand and served by the Son, from whom we receive the precious gifts and fruits of the Spirit of love. The ingredient of the eucharist is no less than Christ himself, from whom we draw the fullness of life and all the necessary strength required, for our mission of bringing him to others.

The love of God, however, has made the eucharist even more than a meal by which we are fed and sustained spiritually: it is also the sacrament of solidarity – for it is the real presence of Emmanuel, God always with us and at our side! It unites our human living with the endless life of God, by making us one with that sacrifice by which Christ has destroyed our death and restored our life.

The eucharist is the sacrament of gathering into one family, the beloved daughters and sons of God – for just as many grains of wheat are required to form a single loaf, and countless grapes to produce one vintage – so all of us together are needed by God to be living cells of his presence in the world. We all form a single Body in Christ, for as we share the same supper, a common energy of love is generated, which empowers us to be the family of God.

Although we are many, we are, in fact, motivated by that one force of superabundant life and limitless love to be found in Christ. We are like countless sparks of one fire, sent to brighten the darkness of lives which no longer know, or have never known, the warmth of God's touch. And because we are light in the world, bearers of God's compassion for the people created and loved by him, we must be always tapped into the source of that fathomless love.

'Cut off from me you can do nothing!' says Christ. That is why the eucharist is the fount and summit of our Christian discipleship. It is the well-spring of our vitality. It provides the impetus, the 'get up and go' that is essential if our mission to others is to be effective in bearing much fruit of lives changed, of sinners reconciled, of the broken and crushed, revived and restored.

The eucharist is the sacrament of companionship. It is the abiding presence of God who loves our company – who is consumed with love for us – whose delight is to be in communion with us. If the eucharistic celebration is at the heart of our daily living and the means of our having spiritual life, then the real presence of our Lord in the Blessed Sacrament which remains after Mass, is the opportunity for ongoing communion of our entire being – heart, soul, mind and strength – with him, in this sacramental means by which his love has found an ingenious manner of remaining with us always, until the time is come for the veil to be removed.

Adoration of the Blessed Sacrament is the after-dinner conversation with our dear friend, in which we savour the fullness of life we receive from him in the actual liturgical celebration. The

Blessed Eucharist reserved provides time for us to digest the
word of life spoken by Christ; it allows us to contemplate the sub-
lime reality beneath the sacramental signs.

The eucharist feeds the roots of our apostolate to a people hungry
for substantial spiritual food. As he unites himself with us in the
eucharist, Christ calls us by name and commissions us to go love
and serve in his name. For he comes from the Father's heart to
make him known in the depths of our hearts. As he becomes
present in our inmost selves through the eucharistic food, he re-
plenishes the life of God we received in baptism and confirmation
refuelling the dynamic power of that Spirit who has made our
mortal bodies his dwelling place. Our God is love that is infec-
tious! A consuming fire. Once in the gospel, the Lord declared: 'I
have come to bring fire to the earth and how I wish it were blazing
already!' The work of Jesus Christ was to kindle that fire of God's
warm welcome for human beings, the glow of which sheds radiance on the full revelation of his love for us. Having been drawn
to the Father's heart by Christ, having been enthused and energised in that furnace of the Spirit, we are then invited to be the
sparks and flames of God's hospitality and generosity for all to
whom we are sent.

Christ has given himself in the eucharist, not only for the spiritual
growth of those who follow him, but also for the life of the world;
so that the Church – all who believe – can be an efficient medium
of his loving forgiveness, merciful gentleness and saving justice.
Our having life from him should, therefore, be an advertisement
that will attract others into his friendship. The eucharist is a call to
become, more and more, what we receive – a challenge to allow
Christ to transfigure the substance of our hidden selves so that,
day and daily, we will become more clearly recognisable for our
fellow pilgrims on the journey of life, as signs of the presence of
living God.

The essence of our vocation as a eucharistic people, is to go out to
all our sisters and brothers and share with them the bread of our
companionship; to offer the cup of kindliness and refreshment; to
be bearers of the basin and towel of selfless service.

The eucharist is a cry for justice; it is a demand for an end to oppression. It is the prayer of God who was himself victimised and brutally treated. It is the plea of Christ who was unjustly condemned to a shameful death, who laid down his life and who has now taken it up again forever (Jn 10:17). The eucharist is the reply of God to a hungry world; to a people deprived not only of material bread, but of their very dignity and livelihood.

At the eucharist we proclaim Christ crucified and risen until he comes. Thus at the eucharist, joys and sorrows, tears and laughter, are fused into a common thrust of resurrected strength which compels us to answer the cry of God – to respond to his command for a new civilisation founded upon justice and mercy, truth and love. When we give our assent to God's invitation: 'Come and eat' (Is 55:1-3), we are taking into ourselves that very power of Christ who was dead and who now is alive for ever and ever (Rev 1:17), he whose Spirit is endless life and love which is stronger than death.

Christ says to the disciples: 'Give them something to eat yourselves' (Mt 14:16). He speaks thus so that those who follow him might never be tempted to send away those who are truly in need; or to turn a blind eye to the tears of the heart-broken; or to be deaf to the moans of the afflicted. At Mass, all the anguish and brokenness of the world is gathered up and joined with the sacrifice of Christ, the New Man (Eph 2:15), he who accompanies us amidst the ruins of so many destroyed and shattered lives.

For even in his very silence, God effectively addresses himself to the broken in heart and crushed in spirit. Christ after all, in his passion and death, was harshly dealt with but bore it humbly '... he never opened his mouth, like a lamb that is led to the slaughter-house, like a sheep that is dumb before its shearers never opening its mouth' (Is 53:7).

So too he never opened his mouth but silently confronted the full horror of evil and the awful darkness of death; and in so doing he has brought about the means whereby all things will be made new and every tear, at long last, wiped away. Nothing can come between us and such love; no troubles, no worries, neither height nor depth, nor any power, earthly or otherwise – our trail of tears is transformed into a victorious march by the power of him who loved us (Rom 8:35-37).

The eucharist is a blessing to be shared and celebrated with thanksgiving; it is a sacrifice to be offered and participated in; it is a real presence to be worshipped and adored. It is also, however, a life to be lived; and in order to live a truly eucharistic life, one must be ever ready to receive those who come to us in whatever kind of need – those in need of time, of company, of friendship, love or support. In order to celebrate the eucharist worthily, one we must be tuned into the pain of the world and actively involved in the struggle for a world in communion – a world where all, without exception, will be assured of a place at the table of those benefits, with which God has so richly blessed our earth, for the good of all.

Yes the eucharist is God's demand for such a world: a world that is no longer a lonely place but a habitation of solidarity and friendship. A world where human beings can give thanks together for the gift of life: where God and humanity are in communion and seated together at the table.

CHAPTER SEVEN

Prayer:
Loving a passionate God

Lord, teach us to pray
Now once he was in a certain place praying, and when he had
finished, one of his disciples said, 'Lord teach us how to pray,
just as John taught his disciples' (Lk 11:1).

As they watched him commune with the Father, a chord was
sounded which resonated at the very core of their being, like a
song remembered suddenly from long ago, a snatch of music
once shared when God, the man and the woman, had walked together in the garden in the cool of the day, when humanity was
still warm from the heart of God. Suddenly the songs that are
sung in the house of the Trinity are loud once more in the ears of
humanity, stirring echoes of deep yearnings, in the deep places of
our hearts – those places prepared by God's own hand to be his
private quarters. Lord teach us to pray ...

Jesus Christ is the sheer loving passion of God engaging and pursu-
ing us. He has come to confront us with the reality of a Father who
is waiting for us to come back; a God who so loved the world, that
he could bear to wait no longer, but set off himself into the mist and
darkness of human history, to seek out what had been lost and
carry it home rejoicing. In so doing, he makes himself vulnerable
by sending him who is most precious to him – the only Son who is
nearest the Father's heart – to make him known. In Christ, God has
exposed his heart and allowed it to be broken by humanity – vio-
lently torn asunder by the dark forces that had inhabited human
history and experience, upon our self-imposed exile.

A parent is most vulnerable in its child: to lose a child is the ultimate disaster; to see one's child cruelly killed could indeed be the
death of a mother or father and, certainly, it would be a nightmare
from which it might not be possible to awaken. Yes, on Calvary
the sun grew so dark that many feared it would never rise again.

83

God, in his Son the Incarnate Word, made his heart vulnerable, allowing it to be pierced and broken. And from that heart there came flowing blood and water, in a deluge that swept death away forever! The veil of separation was torn in two and from that broken body and pierced heart, God was able to reach into our pain and darkness and embrace us, speaking to our fears an almighty Word that would reverberate in resurrection. The flood gates of grace are now forever open, God is among us and the joy of the resurrection will renew the whole earth, awakening every heart from the sleep of smug self-satisfaction and the living death of oblivious selfishness. Lord, by your cross and resurrection it is morning once more, the long night of our lost cries and fear haunted sleep is past and we see on our horizon the morning star begin to unfold its radiant splendour: Christ, that morning star, who came back from the dead, and shed his peaceful light on all human-kind.

> ...That is why it is said: Wake up from your sleep, rise from the
> dead and Christ will shine on you (Eph 5:14).

Yes indeed, it seems almost like a dream that the Lord has delivered us from our ancient bondage to the tyranny of death: but we need only to open our eyes and arise, so that the revivifying freshness of the Spirit's breath on Easter morning might assure us that this is no reverie or wishful thinking. The day of songs has dawned forever, such songs as this:

> Alleluia!
> I love the Lord for he listens to my entreaty;
> He bends down to listen to me when I call.
>
> Death's cords were tightening round me,
> the nooses of Sheol (Hell);
> distress and anguish gripped me,
> I called on the Lord's name:
>
> Lord rescue me!
>
> The Lord is righteous and merciful,
> our God is tender-hearted;
> The Lord defends the simple,
> he saved me when I was brought to my knees.
>
> Return to your resting place, my soul,
> The Lord has treated you kindly.

He has rescued me from death
my eyes from tears and my feet from stumbling.
I will walk in the Lord's presence in the land of the living

(Thus) I have faith, even when I say,
'I am completely crushed'.
(When) In my alarm, I declared,
'No one can be relied on.'
(And so) What return can I make to the Lord
For all his goodness to me?
(Ps 116:1-12)

Prayer is the return I make to the Lord for the wonder of love he expresses to me. Prayer is loving God back. That is why Christ says to us:

In your prayers do not babble as the pagans do, for they think that by using many words they will make themselves heard. Do not be like them, your Father knows what you need before you ask him. So you should pray like this:

Our Father in heaven,
may your name be held holy,
your kingdom come,
your will be done,
on earth as in heaven.

Give us our daily bread.
And forgive us our debts,
as we have forgiven those who are in debt to us.

And do not put us to the test,
but save us from the evil one.
(Mt 6:7-13)

The key word in prayer is 'Father': it is not a servile attitude of craven grovelling where it becomes a battle to find as many words as possible, to appease, find favour, plead our case, or twist God's arm. That could never be the case, for prayer is always the action and initiative of the Spirit of love, who lives in our hearts and breathes in our living. Prayer is being and living in love with God, a continuous state of consciousness of his presence, at every moment of one's existence. To pray is a perpetual standing in his presence and walking in his company, much of which will occur in the 'nitty gritty' situations of life, among the 'pots and pans' of each day's journey.

Lord teach us to pray; the disciple, in expressing such a request to the Lord, was articulating the most profound of human needs, the fundamental necessity of being in relationship with the source of our existence. As Augustine's ancient yet timeless wisdom reminds us: we are created for friendship and union with God, so much so, that our hearts will never have any peace until they at last rest in him. Prayer is our reply to the overtures God makes from on high – his reaching down and taking us in his arms, his pressing us against his cheek as one does with an infant, his stooping down and giving us food (*cf* Hosea 11:1-4). Praying is loving God back.

Prayer: Living as God's children

After all, what other return can we possibly make to such a passionate love? (Ps 116:12) One can only accept or refuse: to accept is to reply in the affirmative to God's invitation, to be the person that he created me to be. To pray is to say 'yes' while fully conscious of who I am and who he is. To pray is to face the God who formed me, knitting me together in my mother's womb and to thank him for all these mysteries: for the wonder of myself and all his works (Ps 139:13-14). Prayer is kneeling before the God who made us in an attitude of complete trust, saying yes to who he is, almighty even though we feel small, weak and helpless. To pray is to accept and do the will of God who will never abandon or forsake us. For in asking us to abandon ourselves to him he says:

> Do not be afraid for I am with you; stop being anxious and watchful for I am your God. I give you strength, I bring you help, I uphold you with my victorious right hand ... I am holding you by the right hand; I tell you, do not be afraid, I will help you (Is 41:10-13).

Such is the living word of a God who is faithful, who is passionately in love with us. They are not the sentiments one would expect of a coldly aloof 'unmoved mover' model of deity. Our God is profoundly moved, in his very depths, at the thought of us; for our having life is a revelation in itself, of his dynamic and passionate love. Such is the love which pursues and will not let us go, a love that calls for a response, yes or no. Give in, he pleads; relent; if one of you hears me calling and is moved by my persistent knocking and opens the door, I will come in to share your meal, side by side, with you (Rev 3:20). Our God is a consuming fire (Heb 12:29): a living flame who refashions us in the crucible of his love. Such is the real and living God, who leaps like flame from the living traditions of revelation and sets the lives and experiences of human beings ablaze with his presence.

In response to the disciples request, 'Lord teach us to pray', Jesus replies: 'When you pray, say this: 'Our Father ...' In his life, he showed what it is like to live on intimate terms with God. He has done all the spade work and paved the way for us to draw close and experience the reality of God's love for us, as Father. By becoming one of us, Christ has made us one with him, so that, with him, we can come into the presence of our Creator, with all the confident boldness of children. The beloved disciple, John, overwhelmed at the extent of God's love for us, says to us in utter wonder:

Think of the love that the Father has lavished on us by letting us be called God's children, and that is what we are.

We are children and heirs: qualified through the sheer gift of his grace, to share the inheritance of the saints in light. He set his heart on us before ever the world was, determined that we would be his. He plucked us from the oblivion of nonentity; called us out of the darkness of not knowing who we are or what we are meant to be, and makes it clear that our origins are embedded firmly in his heart, that the roots of our existence draw life from him alone. And now we know that we are a chosen race, a royal priesthood, a consecrated nation, a people set apart to sing the praises of God who called us out of the darkness into his wonderful light. 'Once you were not a people at all and now you are God's people; once you were outside the mercy and now you have been given mercy' (1 Pet 2:9-10).

Praying is living in the knowledge of who we are as God's people. To pray is to live and walk as a daughter, a son, of the God whom we call Father. A God who shares life with us at the deepest level possible; a God who comes to meet us on the holy ground of everyday living; a God who walks our streets and who is really present with us, at the kitchen sink or on the factory floor or wherever we experience life at whatever level. God is with us, never absent for an instant. He vests us with the best robe and puts a ring on our finger and nothing is allowed to strip us of our precious value and dignified bearing in his eyes.

The dynamics of prayer: Making God's presence felt

The good news of our salvation is the truth about who we are – we are loved by God – our human dignity and value is the direct result of his loving us passionately. This is the truth enshrined in and upheld by the Church, in the difficult environment of today's anti-human society. The Christian vision of a truly human society is one which enables people to be fully alive, to be what God created them to be. The vocation, therefore, of every believing and loving person is to be a minister of human dignity. Our work is to uphold and defend, to proclaim and enhance, the truth of each person's relevance, value and the significance of their place in the world. The task of the Christian community is to create a place where all can find their true home. The Church must always labour at becoming the common ground for all humanity, where all can discover their true identity and reality. For that very reason, we, as the family of faith, must know exactly who we are. We must not surrender our dignity to those subtle, and indeed increasingly blatant attempts to plunder it. We must reclaim the value of the afflicted and demand the rights of those trampled on, by the oppressor's many feet.

On World Peace day, 1993, Pope John Paul II made this appeal: 'If you want peace, reach out to the poor.' Throughout the world, and on our streets, it is possible to detect an undeniable relationship between that low self-esteem and poor self-image engendered by the denial of basic human rights and decent employment to generations of families, and that violent unrest which is an increasingly frightful reality, both at local and global level.

There are all too many left destitute in the gutter of a fast moving world; rejects expelled from the 'have-have not' schools of thought. Such a world moves too fast for the unemployed and the poor, for the weak and defenceless, for the old, the sick and the unborn. Human beings are treated with growing contempt; men, women and children are valued only in so far as they contribute; only in so far as they are regular devotees at the many shrines erected to honour the cult of money and pleasure; and only worthwhile in so far as they are suitable fodder for the cannon of consumerism. The human person's rightful place at the heart of creation has been usurped at the whim of market forces and a perverse notion of development.

'If you want peace, reach out to the poor!' Part of reaching out to the modern poor, must be the provision of work that is in keeping with human dignity and rewarded with a just wage. Unemployment spells the slavery of the human spirit, for it means that men and women are deprived of the right to contribute and co-operate freely, for the general good of all. Unemployment is the devastating fall-out from a self-absorbed and heartless society, which conspires against the value of human life, from the womb to the tomb. Unemployment is the sin of those who selfishly manipulate world resources. It is a crime against humanity and a refusal to take seriously the welfare and dignity of human persons, families and communities. 'If you want peace, reach out to the poor!' The world of today is peppered with examples of where anger, despair and sheer frustration is bearing the fruit of bloody conflict and violent uprising.

Who can deliver us from such a climate, save our loving and faithful God, who knows each one by name? Only he, the true shepherd, can rescue us from an environment of affliction, created by anti-human forces and morally redundant philosophies, which have cynically plundered human dignity and mercilessly corroded the value and sanctity of human life.

And herein lies our recovery and our salvation: to stand our ground and not to draw back; to proclaim, loud and clear, I am a man! I am a woman! I am a person! We need to ask ourselves: What sort of people are we? Are we the kind who are going to apologise for our existence? Are we going to swallow the lie that our value lies only in what we own? How much we earn? What we do? Are we going to bow down before the idolatrous falsehoods, that enslave and tyrannise so many, in this day and age?

I believe that the answer is a resounding No! We owe it to no one to justify our existence. God, who loves us passionately and unconditionally, has given us our life and our dignity. The author of the letter to the Hebrews leaves us under no misapprehension as to what our stance should be: 'You and I are not the sort of people who draw back and are lost by it; we are the sort who keep faithful until our souls are saved' (Heb 10:39).

The God who walks our streets, counts on us to make his presence felt and such action for justice is the fruit of genuine prayer and real relationship with God. That is why he charges us at the end of the Mass: 'Go in peace to love and serve!' For the eucharist, of course, is never really over because our companion never retires from our midst: 'You must live your whole life according to the Christ you have received – Jesus the Lord; you must be rooted in him and built on him and held firm by the faith you have been taught, and over-flowing with thanksgiving' (Col 2:6-7).

Because the God we worship is infinite and uncontainable, so too prayer defies definitive analysis. If prayer really is friendship with God, then just like human love and relationship, it will permeate every pocket of my life. No one decides, for example, to be married for only so many hours a day; or to be someone's friend only at weekends. Friendship with God is the same. Prayer is allowing the real presence of God to saturate my entire life. It is to live in the spirit of 'Patrick's breastplate', 'Christ with me, Christ within me, Christ behind me, Christ before me ...' It is to be conscious that everything is grace, and grace is everywhere; for all of life's reality, even what is distasteful and unpleasant, is touched, imbued and aflame with God's nearness. He has graced us with his presence at every moment of our lives.

Prayer thus, is not so much a matter of many words or even long hours but is a whole attitude of life: a manner of being, aptly described by St John of the Cross as 'loving attentiveness to God.' Such loving attentiveness to God must of course be expressed in loving attentiveness to those around me. Practical charity is always the acid test of the quality of prayer and the state of my relationship with God. Prayer is the means by which we remain in Christ's love, firmly rooted in him who is the true vine producing in us the fruit of his own goodness and love (cf Jn 15:1-17; 1 Jn 4:20).

There is a real human need to, as we say in the North of Ireland, 'get your head showered.' The God who made us knows this to be the case; and so the Lord invites us: 'Come aside and rest a little' (Mk 6:31). He also says: 'When you pray go into your private room, shut yourself in and pray to your Father who is in that secret place' (Mt 6:6). That secret place can be many things. For some, the silence of the Church before the Blessed Sacrament; for others, a quiet space in the house or even a corner of the bedroom; for others still, a walk in the countryside or even a journey on the bus!

However, there is one ultimate secret place and that is the space God has carved out for himself with his own hand – that empty space within our own depths. It is there, above all, that God wishes to reclaim his own ground: it is these restless hearts of ours that he wishes to make still, at peace and rest in him alone.

CHAPTER EIGHT

Mary:
Transfigured humanity personified

Mary's significance in our faith story

The family of faith has always celebrated a unique relationship with Mary, who exercises her ministry as a role-model for God's people, embodying maternal and sisterly charisms. In the midst of that great cloud of witnesses on every side of us (Heb 12:1), she is immediately distinguishable as the one whose light shines most brightly. The disciples recognise their mother at once, for the heart is instinctively drawn in the direction of one whose faith and love are living legend, for all generations. We see too, in Mary, the image of what we are becoming; an image suffused with colours that reflect the invisible light of him who will perform spectacular marvels of grace for us also, if we will allow him.

Mary is the most striking model of faith, hope and love, lived out in trustful obedience. However, if she is to speak with full voice to the man and woman of today, she must be liberated from the mould of plaster and plastic, with which reactionary piety has surrounded her. Mary wishes to be free to point towards her son and to tell us: Do whatever he tells you (Jn 2:6). It is a shame that her arm should be restrained by certain types of Marian devotion and spirituality, which encircle her with a rosy haze of cloying sweetness and unattainable ideals.

Mary exemplifies, in the entirely of her being, the unbreakable bond established between God and humanity and cemented in the Word made flesh. As Irenaeus, the great leader and teacher of the young Church has put it: 'The glory of God is humanity fully alive.' Mary, in her glorified womanhood, is the prototype of our being fully alive in Christ which will find its ultimate expression at the wedding feast in the kingdom of the Trinity.

It is in this context that the icon of Mary becomes tangible and her ideals attainable. The great truths about Mary, virgin, mother and woman, need to be exposed to our contemporary atmosphere, for they shed further light on our true identity as the people among whom Emmanuel has made his home; the people with whom God is a fellow pilgrim on our way to the kingdom.

Ever since the disciple made a place for her in his home, Mary has been in the midst of the family of faith, exercising an effective ministry of continuous prayer (Jn 19:27; Acts 1:14). Indeed, the image of Mary is indelibly printed on the very heart of the Church. The description of Mary as virgin, mother and woman is a positively affirmative statement about the human person. For example, the fact that Mary is venerated as ever-virgin, owes nothing to any negative or prohibitive view of human sexuality. Rather, it is a profound statement about the manner in which our passionate and loving creator approaches our delicate humanity. As with the image of the burning bush (Ex 3:1-6), he is able to be present without consuming or violating. Our God is infinite dynamic of loving passion, yet his manner is courteous, his voice is gentle as silence, his touch is all tenderness.

Mary's virginity is not for the purpose of removing her from the rest of mortals. Rather, it is a sacrament of her innocence and openness to God; a visible sign of her frank honesty and integrity before and with him; a charism of her energetic and wholehearted willingness to embrace the mystery of God and thus show forth to all generations the eternal uncreated One, who becomes visible and touchable in our midst as, in every sense, the fruit of her womb.

One of the most ancient expressions we have of how the Christian community understands Mary and her particular role in God's saving designs, is the title which describes her as the 'New Eve.' This concept has its roots in the second century: Irenaeus' imagery in particular, is timeless and useful for the insight it gives into the mystery of salvation as: *'a reversal of the original evil along the same path as it had come.'* Irenaeus, in his famous articulation of Christian truth, *Against the heresies*, describes Mary's part in God's saving activities: 'The knot of Eve's disobedience was untied by Mary's obedience; for what Eve bound by her unbelief, Mary loosed by her faith' (*Adv. Haer.* XXII, 4). This image of Mary as a second Eve is a development of Paul's doctrine in Romans which

acclaims Jesus Christ as the new Adam: 'Just as by one man's disobedience many were made sinners, so by one man's obedience
many are made righteous' (cf Rom 5:12-21).

In the twilight of humanity's long night, 'The man named his wife
'Eve' because she was the mother of all those who live.' In the unfolding light of that long awaited hour, when the Son of Man is
lifted up from the earth, there stands at the foot of the cross a
woman: 'Seeing his mother and the disciple he loved standing
near her, Jesus said to his mother, 'Woman this is your son.' Then
to the disciple he said, 'This is your mother' (Jn 19:26-27).

On the morning of recreation, the infant Church would open its
eyes and recognise the sign of a mother; a symbol of the Church itself, in its mission of nursing and nurturing within humanity, the
seed of transfiguration glory. In giving the disciple to Mary as her
son and Mary to the disciple as mother, Jesus calls into being a
new family of believing disciples. The vocation given to Mary is
motherhood: mother of the Word made flesh; mother of all who
accept him in faith and who thus are given the power to become
children of God. Since our belief is in him who was born, not out
of human stock or urge of the flesh or will of man, but of God himself, we therefore are generated into that fullness of life in the family circle of the Trinity (cf Jn 1:12-13). Through the human flesh of
Mary, on account of her saying 'yes' to God in faith, God has
drawn near to the human family and gathered us to himself, in an
eternal embrace of loving passion.

Her presence at the foot of the cross, when the Lord's saving work
is consummated, is of immense significance. She who gave birth
to the saviour, is present also at the birth of the Church, which is
called the Body of Christ and which makes his saving mission
present in the world until the end of the ages. Because of Mary's
complicity, therefore, all people of faith can regard her as blessed
forever; and we can truly say in union with her: The almighty has
done great things for me, holy is his name!

The vocation of Mary, handmaid of the Lord
However, Mary, in spite of the favour she found in God's sight
and the lofty heights to which her vocation had exalted her, was
as much in need of God's grace as any of the rest of us. All her
faith and goodness were the direct result of God's hand at work in

her. She has nothing to boast of in herself, as she categorically states: 'He has looked on his handmaid in her nothingness.' It is only because God did great things for her that all generations will call her blessed. Mary's canticle, the *Magnificat*, sings of the fact that God's grace alone makes her what she is. This is made obvious also upon her meeting with Elizabeth. She is greeted as mother of the Lord and, most blessed of all women; and it is at that moment that a song springs from the depths of her being, returning all praise and thanks to him who is its proper end.

The Mary who emerges from the scriptures is a woman of profound and unique faith. She did not hesitate to take up the divine challenge, in spite of her human uncertainty as to what all this could possibly mean and how it would all work out. She was deeply disturbed by the angels words, yet she asked for no safeguards or explanations. She replied out of that single-minded commitment to God which had been characteristic of her life thus far: 'I am the handmaid of the Lord, let what you have said be done to me.' Such a response was born out of a most remarkable faith and love, for she had always heard God's word and kept it. She pondered the mystery of her Son and treasured it in her heart; a heart that would be pierced frequently with that unique sorrow known to mothers. She would have much to suffer, as she struggled to fathom the depths of this child, who would be fire on earth from the Father's heart.

Almost all of our scriptural encounters with Mary are moments and times of trial and distress. The very circumstances of the Lord's conception and birth were highly stressful. God's plan for her however was not that she face her trials in isolation; for she was betrothed to a man named Joseph of the house of David. Joseph is taken from the wings and led, almost reluctantly, centre stage in the great drama of salvation. He is well described in the gospel of Matthew as a man of honour. We could not wish for a more detailed portrait of Joseph than what can be gleaned from the pages of the gospels. He is portrayed as gentle, courageous, sensitive and caring toward his fiancée. In other events, the quiet carpenter is revealed as a man of not merely physical strength. Above all, he is finely tuned to the whisper of the Spirit, who always turns his steps in the right direction.

He had made up his mind to divorce her informally, to spare her shameful exposure to a public who could never understand. It is not that he thought her unfaithful; he knew all too well, the beauty of the holiness with which God's grace had bedecked her. It was not her he doubted but himself. Perhaps Elizabeth's words were ringing in his ears: 'Why should I be honoured with a visit from the mother of my Lord?' He wondered if he was totally out of his depth.

When human beings come face to face with the nearness of God, they invariably hesitate and tremble. There is, however, a chorus that recurs constantly throughout all the accounts of God's drawing close to humanity: it is heard now by Joseph, 'Do not be afraid! Do not be afraid to take Mary home as your wife ...' As human beings, we tend to resemble timid children in our approach to God when he, as Father, wants nothing more than to press us close to his cheek. So do not be afraid Joseph: you are not an intruder on the set; you must take your place along side your wife and give a name and a home to the Word made flesh. For God is determined to speak once more with humanity, as one of the family, face to face.

There, in that relative backwater, that 'one horse town' of Nazareth, Christ lived as a member of a family and local community, for thirty years. There at Nazareth, the Word is made flesh: growing and developing, learning and playing, exploring and living. Unknown. Obscure. Enveloped in the silence and simplicities of daily life and work, in the company of his parents, relatives and neighbours.

Nazareth! Later Nathaniel would wonder: 'Can anything good come out of that place?' Yet in the very silence of Nazareth, God is speaking. Out of the ordinariness of Nazareth, unobtrusively and without spectacle, something quite marvellous is beginning to unfold. The contemplative whisper in the household of Jesus, Mary and Joseph, will crescendo in a mighty cry of deliverance, when God emerges at last from obscurity to comfort his people: *'The Spirit of the Lord has been given to me for the Lord has anointed me. He has sent me to bring good news to the poor, to proclaim liberty to captives and to the blind new sight, to set the down-trodden free, to proclaim the Lord's year of favour '* (Lk 4:18).

Yes! God speaks now in Nazareth, announcing the good news
with irrepressible joy and fervour.

Joseph and Mary, of course, were to hear it first; and it was this
mystery, hidden for generations and centuries (Col 1:26), that
they pondered in their hearts. The vocation of Joseph and Mary
together both mirrors and sheds light on our own calling. Mary,
who by God's grace is the New Eve, already personifies our
human nature made perfect; and Joseph, in his quiet and dignified
manner, shows us what it means for human beings to take their
courage in their hands and agree to co-operate wholeheartedly
with the creator Father. Joseph and Mary together are given the
task of making it possible for Christ to become present in the
world, thus allowing our unseen God to have an inroad into the
visible realities of human experience and living. Mary, overshad-
owed by the creator Spirit, gives birth to the creator Son; and
Joseph takes his place at her side so that the Almighty, who approaches us empty-handed and in utter poverty, might be able to
have a name, a family, a home eventually, and relative security
for a time.

Such is the mission of the workers of Nazareth. By their epic faith
and immense love they, on behalf of all generations, prepare a
suitable cradle for the birth of him, the hope of the nations (Gen
49:10). They graciously allow God to be employed at last, in exe-
cuting his heart's dearest wish – the great saving work accomplished in his Son's birth, life, death and resurrection. When one
contemplates the family life of Jesus, Mary and Joseph at Nazareth, one can only but be overcome with awe; for here we stand on
the threshold of God's dwelling place and we behold the infinite
mystery of God's love for us made really present in our midst.
The paschal mystery begins to unfold in all its dazzling array.

The sign of a woman: Icon of humanity fully alive
The song of Mary, her Magnificat, is a great shout of thanksgiving, but it is also a cry she makes on behalf of the poor of this
earth. Mary speaks up as the champion of the oppressed, her
words will send the high and mighty toppling from their seats.
She is expressing on behalf of all generations the profound gratitude that we owe to our Creator on account of his saving help.

That saving help is no longer a distant hope. Now Mary is conscious of it as a real presence in her womb, a child who is growing
and developing – a little one not yet born who is formed in the
depths of her being.

This image of the Virgin Mother has always been the cause of
great happiness for the Christian people. Indeed we call our Lady
the cause of our joy. Her profound faith and open-hearted generosity will allow the Word of God to take root in her, so that she
becomes pregnant, by the power of the Holy Spirit, with her
Creator.

Mary is, at one and the same time, ever-virgin and truly Mother of
God; for nothing is impossible to God who raises those who co-
operate with him to eternal possibilities. Yes indeed, there is no
limiting what he who is almighty can do for those who, in wonder
and awe, allow themselves to be led by him. Mary's virginity
characterises her relationship with God: she loves him utterly; her
approach to God is marked by a true innocence and purity of
heart. Although she was deeply disturbed and asked herself what
the angel's greeting could mean, she remains candid and tranquil
in the presence of the mystery of God; she doesn't take flight; she
asks the angel questions for further clarification of what God is expecting of her. By no means does she receive any assurance that
this task will be easy; God is honest and open with her as she is
with him. She who enjoyed God's favour, and who thus far obviously, in her young life had devoured the words of the living
God, would have been intimately attuned to the message of scripture about the promised Christ and the path of suffering he would
accept on our behalf. Yet, courageously, she consecrates herself
totally to what is asked of her: *'You see before you the Lord's servant,
let it happen to me as you have said'* (cf. Lk 1:26-38).

*The Holy Spirit will come upon you and the power of the Most High will
cover you with its shadow.* From the depths of her purity and generous open-heartedness, the Creator Spirit brings forth the Holy
One of God – the long expected Messiah – who saves his brothers
and sisters from their sins and brings them home to the Father.
She is therefore, truly Mother of God the Eternal Word made
flesh. The Holy Spirit thus causes motherhood to blossom out of
her virginal purity and innocence of heart, crowning her woman-

hood with even greater dignity. She gives birth to her Son and calls him Jesus; and to those who believe in his name and accept him, he gives power to become children of God (Jn 12-13). Mary, who at the beginning of his life presents him to the world (Mt 2:11), is present at every painful step of that process of crucifixion leading to glorification, by which the Church comes to birth.

The journey to Calvary begins when he is a little child. The cross looms on the horizon ominously. Rachel's bitter lamenting and weeping bewails its inevitability (Mt 2:16-18). We can scarcely begin to fathom the extent to which Mary shared with her Son in his deep distress (cf. Lk 12:49-50), to see kindled, with the wood of the cross, that fire of the Love of God, the blaze of which obliterates death; and which casts a new lustre on our humanity in the light of which we realise that we are children of God. At that great moment when the Son of Man is lifted up from the earth, we see Mary closely associated with his suffering and profoundly identified with his actions for the salvation of the world.

And now we stand in the full radiance of the dawn from on high; the old order gives way to the new and there stands on the horizon of the new heaven and the new earth, a woman: 'Woman, this is your son. And to the disciple he said, This is your mother.' And from that moment the disciple made a place for her in his home.

Throughout all her dark trials and sorrows, Mary emerges at last as the woman of faith *par excellence*. A woman bathed in the radiant light of the risen Christ, the image of humanity transfigured. For such reasons, the disciples take their mother to their heart; a special place has been prepared in the household of faith that will always be hers, as the model of faith and commitment that must be characteristic of a disciple. She is the mother of all those who live by faith. She is the living image of all that awaits us at the goal of our pilgrimage. She is our own flesh and blood and already we see in her a vision of our humanity as it is meant to be and can be, when its substance of frailty and mortality is transfigured by an eternal Word, into the substance of endless risen life. Mary's humanity is now entirely invested with the colours of glory chosen for us by the Father and woven into the fabric of our being by the Lord's cross and resurrection. This is the marvellous truth expressed in her immaculate conception and assumption.

The theology of Mary's immaculate conception and her assumption is a hymn inspired by the Spirit of truth, which celebrates the victory of Christ and proclaims the triumph of God's grace, at work in our wounded and fallen humanity. They were not conjured up out of nowhere. Rather, their definition by the Church was a result of the insinuations of the Holy Spirit throughout the ages, as the wonderful truth about Jesus Christ began to really hit home with the family of faith as they reflected more and more on that evolving and unfolding truth. Christ himself had intimated to his apostles that this would be possible when he said to them:

> I still have many things to say to you but they would be too much for you now. But when the Spirit of truth comes he will lead you to the complete truth, since he will not be speaking as from himself but will only say what he has learnt; and he will tell you of the things to come (Jn 16:13).

There is in theology what is called a hierarchy of truths, of primary and secondary doctrines. The primary and basic doctrines of Christianity concern God and Christ. On the basis of these primary or most important teachings, there unfold other secondary doctrines which we hold to be true as logical follow through of what goes before. You could perhaps say that the secondary doctrines of the Christian faith are the blossom and fruit generated by its essential and basic dogma. In the case of Mary, for example, the primary doctrine expresses the truth that Jesus Christ, true God and true man, is born of her and that truly, therefore, she is the mother of God. As a result of her being mother of the Lord, other things are true of her. We believe that in order to give birth to Christ, the sinless one, she herself, by God's grace, would need to be free from all trace of sin. It was both possible and appropriate for God to preserve her from the original sin and the possibility of actual sin. This is what God did for her from the first instant of her conception; it was appropriate that he do so on account of her mission to give birth to him who would save his people from their sins. It was possible to do so because Christ's saving work and his redemptive death cannot be limited to a moment in time, even though he suffered and died at a place called Golgotha, at a particular period in human history. That moment however, was always present in God's plan of salvation for the human race. The

grace given to Mary by God, therefore, in the immaculate conception, is the direct result of her Son's redemptive sacrifice and his
merits alone as saviour of the world. To Mary, in a unique manner, can Paul's teaching be particularly applied:

> Blessed be God the Father of Our Lord Jesus Christ, who has
> blessed us with all the spiritual blessings of heaven in Christ.

> Before the world was made, he chose us, chose us in Christ, to
> be holy and spotless and to live through love in his presence,
> determining that we should become his adopted sons and
> daughters through Jesus Christ for his own kind purposes, to
> make us praise the glory of his grace, his free gift to us in the
> beloved.

> And it is in him that we were claimed as God's own, chosen
> from the beginning, under the predetermined plan of the one
> who guides all things as he decides by his own will; chosen to
> be, for his greater glory, the people who would put their hopes
> in Christ before he came (Eph 1:3-3; 11-12).

Mary's grace of the immaculate conception is of great consequence
for humanity, for it celebrates our value as human beings. She too,
like us, had to be saved by God's grace. He accomplished this for
her, at the first moment of her existence, not for her own glorification but so that all might see his glory revealed in every generation. In preserving her from sin, he was equipping her for special
work, but that does not mean that she had an easier time of it than
other mortals – the very opposite is true! She experienced temptation in all its fury and severity as well as every conceivable
emotional upheaval and trauma of human living. Yet so intense
was her faith and so profound the depth of her love that she was
able to keep pace with her Son, even though she did not always
understand him.

Mary's love for God and her openness to his plans bore fruit in
Christ, who is come to seek out and save what was lost (Lk 19:10).
Her faith and love open the door for God to come among us and
reclaim us as his lost property. That is why her immaculate conception and assumption are a triumph for every human being.
The mother of God is the splendid example of what God's grace
does in a human person. She reflects the brightness of his glory
into our darkness. Her 'yes' provokes the 'yes' of countless others.

She cuts a regal figure among the people of God and is honoured as the first lady of the new creation, for when the Word became flesh and was born of Mary, the possibility of endless life was born also. Mary's acceptance of her mission: 'I am the handmaid of the Lord, let what you have said be done to me', is the occasion of every generation from now onwards calling her blessed, for what she had actually done was to, on behalf of all people of faith, pave the way for the resurrection and open the door for us onto the restoration and renewal of all things in Jesus Christ, the fruit of her womb. Thus Mary's assumption directs our gaze toward the horizon of glory. It keeps ever in our mind our true homeland in heaven. The sight of Mary's glorified humanity keeps ever green our own hope, for the day when the Lord Jesus will trans-figure these bodies of ours into copies of his glorious risen body (Phil 3:20-21). Mary is a symbol of hope for the pilgrim faithful, as we journey from exile to homeland. What God has done for Mary, he is doing for us. By his grace and love, we have a remedy for sin and the sure hope of eternal life, through Jesus Christ.

The doctrine of the immaculate conception was defined a truth of the faith in 1854 and the assumption in 1950. Obviously the Church did not dream up these teachings within the last hundred odd years. They had been part of what is called *consensus fidelium* since the earliest times. The *consensus fidelium* is the instinctive faith of the people that something believed is true. The doctrines of the immaculate conception and assumption had been widely believed since about the third century. In 1854 and 1950, the teach-ing authority of the Church articulated and presented them for all time as truths of the faith. It is possible to do this on account of what is called the development of doctrine. Doctrine develops and evolves because the Christian tradition is a living one; it is the Spirit 'who explores the depths of everything even the depths of God' (1 Cor 2:10), who breathes within the community of faith and leads us into the complete truth (Jn 16:13).

As time went on, the Christian community reflected on and stud-ied the truth of Christ in order to focus it more accurately. It became necessary to reiterate what was believed in the face of errors, distortions and falsehood. That is where we get our creeds from; they are statements of belief by the early Church, drawn up to refute heresy and counteract wrong interpretations of the Christian message. This involved a process of drawing out more of the truth contained in the primary doctrines of Christianity, and so there occurs a gradual unfolding of truth in all its many facets yet all reflecting the one light. This development is steered clear of contradiction and kept out of doctrinal cul-de-sac by the direct guidance of the Holy Spirit acting through the charisms of the Church's pastoral and teaching authority and the consensus of God's people.

Therefore, the doctrines of the immaculate conception and assumption are simply further developments, following on from and as a result of, the truth of Christ who saves us from sin and who, by placing us within the community of faith, raises us to the fullness of life by making us living members of his body.

Our devotion to Mary is born out of the maternal and sisterly affection we experience from the mother of God. Our love for her and her love for us has its source in our common love for him who is the only saviour and the sole mediator. We are glad with Mary for, in her, God's sovereign grace has already triumphed. In the mystery of salvation, she is one who gives the invisible God the opportunity to be seen, heard and touched, in the wonder of the Christ event. Her role, in the life of a disciple, is to be a motherly example and a source of encouragement in our own particular struggles and trials. She watches over us like an elder sister, on our pilgrimage of faith. Always she indicates her Son and advises: 'Do whatever he tells you'. She keeps before our eyes an awareness that our mission too is to be vehicles of revelation; instruments of God's compassionate love and bearers of the new wine of joy, which irrigates our living with the utter fullness of God and inebriates our humanity with the precious gifts of the Spirit. We too, with Mary, have a vocation to make the invisible visible in our lives. For our humanity is already pregnant with a glory that will one day be revealed, when it unfurls in the kingdom of eternal communion, as the wedding garment of life in its fullness.

'For our God is a consuming fire.'
(Heb 12:29)

The believer is one in whose heart burns divine fire; the one who hopes, has eyes for the invisible presence of God who reaches into the very depths of our existence. Those who love, allow the Word to become flesh and blood in them, drawing others into his burning embrace. Faith is that divine fire cast upon the earth by the risen Christ whenever he passed beyond our sight, 'not to abandon us but to be our hope' (*Preface of the Ascension I*). The light of faith renders the invisible knowable: it is a bright cloud which veils the splendour of God for we are not as yet fully grown and capable of such sights. In the meantime, it is enough to believe, to hope and to love.

Jesus Christ has sown within us the seeds of glory which will bear the harvest of life to the full (Jn 10:10). 'Whoever believes in me will never die,' says Christ. It is not possible to destroy this fullness of life that is the essence of God. Death has always tried and failed; that is why it turned its full fury on the Son of God in his passion and death. They plotted his downfall, whispered plans in backrooms: 'How will we catch him? Where will he be next Wednesday? Here is the scheme whereby we will finish him forever!' They caught him in their net and dealt with him viciously, cutting him down in his youthful vigour, as have been so many since. For his part, he made no resistance, neither did he turn away. He offered his back to those who struck him, his cheeks to those who tore at his beard; he did not cover his face against insult and spittle. The Lord God comes to his help, so that he is untouched by the insults. So too, he sets his face like flint; he knows he shall not be shamed (Is 50:5-7).

They killed him and sealed him up in a dark tomb. Death and its minions danced on his grave. In the depths of that blackness, however, the seed of life eternal began to germinate and take root;

it began to recreate out of the dust and nothingness of the cold grave. Life wrestled and grappled with the dark and chill soil, moistened by the sweat and tears of countless generations of Adam and Eve's off-spring. On the third day, it could no longer be contained but burst forth: I am the Resurrection...! Death therefore has no power over him any more. It has tried and failed. Christ has come back to us from the dead and his endless life overflows into ours through the sacraments.

In baptism we died with Christ ... Does not that statement always ring strange in our ears? It means that when we are baptised, it is somewhat like taking a dip in those living waters of the fullness of life. In that bath we are washed clean and death that lurks within us is drowned. In baptism we die to death; the grip of death on our humanity is prized open, by the strong arm of Christ crucified and risen. At baptism, Christ's own life becomes ours, so that we are actually reborn as God's own beloved daughters and sons. That life is continuously sustained, renewed, confirmed, replenished, revitalised and re-ordered as Christ meets us throughout our earthly lives in the sacraments. Above all, in the eucharist it is constantly strengthened, so that when our physical lives in these mortal bodies come to an end, we are strong enough to leap into God's presence and enjoy life to the full.

On the day of Pentecost, the risen Christ let loose once more in the history of human beings, that creator Spirit who has spoken through the prophets; yet who now, through Christ, makes a home in the hearts of men and women of faith. This is the Spirit who falls on the disciples like a consuming fire; and suddenly, in that vibrant burst of divine energy, their eyes are opened and they realise what it is they must do: for that Pentecostal fire is the light of faith. They stand up in the marketplace and speak of the marvels of God. The Church – the family of faith – is born! For God, in Jesus, has wedded the human race for ever; and through this one Spirit of Father and Son, all peoples will be able to hear a harmonious voice, which will sing forever of life's march over death, love's victory over hate, hope's triumph over despair.

This is a message which will arouse the hostility and opposition of many who will be none too happy that God has so drastically interfered in human affairs of life and death. And so, those who

believe receive from Christ the gift of that peace which no troubles or hardships can take from them. 'Peace be with you' says the
risen Lord, and he showed them his hands and his side (Jn. 20:20).
To reassure them, he makes it clear that, yes, these scars are for
real. Death has been dealt with and those wounds, which spelt
suffering and death for Jesus Christ, are now the means whereby
we can experience flowing upon us, peace, like a river – the breath
of the Spirit who fills the universe with God's presence and who
raises our mortal bodies to glory.

The Spirit of the Lord opens our eyes to the mystery of God and
teaches us that God can never be understood or known in any
earthly or material way. The breath of the Spirit, that mighty
wind, sets us on course into the unknown, where the love of God
burns with an invisible flame, where his heart pulsates with a hidden energy of undying Life.

The work of the Church – your work and my work – is to make
that life of the unseen God present in our world, to be a means
whereby the influence of the Spirit can be felt. The Holy Spirit
achieves her purpose when we place ourselves at her disposal.
For we have all received countless gifts which will be most useful
in our task. Many gifts but one Spirit; it is the same Spirit working
in all of us, 'one Spirit has been given to us all to drink' (1 Cor
12:12-13). Just as we all fill our lungs with the same air, so the one
Spirit is able to work through our many limbs and to use our different voices in proclaiming the gospel of the wonders God has
done in the sight of all the nations.

For though there are many languages in the world, they all com-
municate the same basic hopes and fears of men and women; they
all speak of joys and sorrows, ups and downs, successes and failures. The good news of salvation sings of the fact that God has addressed all these issues, in sending us his only Son. He, Christ, has
dealt with all of them in his passion, death and glorification. He
has gone to the root of the problem – the sin and shame of the
world which resulted in death – and has solved it by becoming
our forgiveness and our peace. The work that we who believe
must be about, is pointing by the way we live, act and speak, towards him, the Lamb of God, who takes away the sin of the world
(Jn 1:29-30). Our salvation is accomplished when we acknowledge

that we are, as human beings, defective and wounded and when we expose ourselves to God's remedy – the free and unmerited gift of his Son's saving companionship. 'Thanks be to God for his inexpressible gift!' (2 Cor 9:15)

The entire mystery of salvation is simply that God loves us, that he wants us to be with him and to work with him. The risen Christ can lead us through our experiences of suffering and brokenness and even defeat, into the fullness of hope and life. The kiss of the Spirit will cleanse our wounds and the Father's embrace will heal them. The Spirit, who breathes and prays in us, makes us fit for our journey towards the kingdom and for the mission of leading people through death and dying, into the new creation.

The Act of Faith impregnates our mortality with divine possibilities and potential. Nothing is impossible to God and there is nothing he cannot accomplish in the person who lives by faith; no work beyond him to achieve, with the help of their hands. God has touched our humanity and filled our living with his breath. The crisp freshness of an Easter morning breeze will not cease to vent itself upon the human spirit, to caress and then to buffet, to assail and then to soothe, but above all to revive and reinvigorate. The world can be filled with the Father's voice resounding in our lives as we allow the Word to go on being made flesh in our flesh. The blaze of the Spirit will open our eyes to what has to be done. Through the hearts of all who believe, our God will continue to make his presence felt; to make sparks of his glory fly – that glory which is man and woman fully alive!

'Let us keep our eyes fixed on Jesus who leads us in our faith and brings it to perfection' (Heb 12:2). In Christ, our humanity recognises itself and discovers itself, as God always knew it to be. In the light of faith and accompanied by the risen Christ, the journey of life is no longer an aimless meandering, but a voyage of discovery, an adventure of love, an exploration of mystery in which we eventually arrive forever at the face of the real and living God, and so are filled with his utter fullness in love (Eph 3:19). To Christ, the Father has entrusted the future of the world and our future. It is he who walks beside us now, Emmanuel; and he who awaits us at the end of the ages.

In Christ we discover our true beauty; we hear from his lips the gracious words which spell the truth of who we are. From him, we gain the confidence and courage to be the persons God created us to be. Let us keep our eyes fixed on him (Lk 4:20). For in him a new age has dawned, the long reign of sin is ended, a broken world has been renewed and we are once again made whole (*Preface of Easter IV*). We, each of us, are his partners and fellow workers, in that joyful employment of constructing the kingdom. Together with him, we are the architects of the new heavens and the new earth; for in our hearts has the creator Spirit made her home; in our lives she breaths and sings – she who is ever renewing the face of the earth!